HARD-WON
WISDOM

HARD-WON WISDOM

ADVICE FOR A RICHER LIFE FROM THE GREATEST GENERATION

Susan Arrington Madsen
Ruth Harris Swaner

Susan Arrington Madsen
Ruth Harris Swaner

DESERET
BOOK
Salt Lake City, Utah

The photographs in this volume are used by permission, courtesy of the following:

Craig Law—5, 13, 29, 31, 37, 45, 47, 53, 55, 79, 91, 95, 97, 107, 113, 121, 127, 131, 141, 143, 145, 153.

Jonathan Swinton—7, 11, 43, 57, 63, 81, 105, 123, 129, 133, 161, 165.

Jenny Johnson—viii, 19, 87, spine.

Individuals or their families—9, 15, 17, 21, 23, 25, 27, 33, 35, 41, 49, 59, 61, 71, 73, 75, 77, 83, 85, 99, 101, 109, 111, 117, 119, 125, 135, 137, 139, 149, 151, 157, 163.

Poem by Spencer H. Smith, page viii, is used by permission, courtesy of his family.

Visit us at DeseretBook.com

Library of Congress Cataloging-in-Publication Data

Hard-won wisdom : advice for a richer life from the greatest generation /
[edited by] Susan Arrington Madsen, Ruth Harris Swaner.
p. cm.
Includes index.
ISBN-13: 978-1-59038-646-0 (hardbound : alk. paper)
ISBN-10: 1-59038-646-9 (hardbound : alk. paper)
1. Conduct of life. 2. Mormons—Conduct of life. 3. Mormons—Interviews.
I. Madsen, Susan Arrington. II. Swaner, Ruth Harris.
BJ1581.2.H275 2007
248.4'89332—dc21 2006033408

Printed in the United States of America
Publishers Printing, Salt Lake City, UT

10 9 8 7 6 5 4 3 2 1

When a person dies,

it is as if an entire library has burned down.

—Alex Haley

Contents

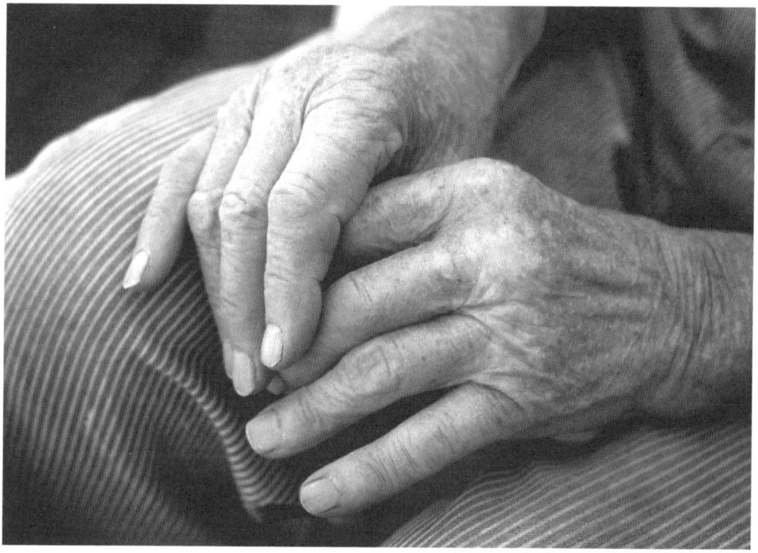

Grandpa's Hands

SPENCER H. SMITH
GRANDSON OF JESSE JACOB ZOLLINGER

Awake early—
The sky still filled with stars,
My feet feel cold on the hard floor.
I say a prayer and walk out to meet the rain.
Lift apples into a bucket,
Not caring for worm holes or frost scars.
Somehow these twisted branches remind me of Grandpa's hands.

Introduction

"WITH THE ANCIENT IS WISDOM; AND IN LENGTH OF DAYS UNDERSTANDING."—JOB 12:12

The wisdom and understanding found in this book come from people who live all around us. The source might be the retired schoolteacher across the street who volunteers at a local elementary school; the World War II veteran who always plants a huge vegetable garden and gives away seemingly truckloads of corn and tomatoes to his lucky friends and neighbors; the kindly sister who greets you at the temple every month; the elderly couple who walk past your home every morning, occasionally picking up a piece of litter along the roadside.

These remarkable souls form a part of our society we call "the elderly." Like magnificent trees, they have weathered and withstood decades of blustery storms, hard knocks, and pesky disease to bless our lives with their wisdom. When asked, they quietly offer a story or two for what they're worth, never expecting praise, honor, or even a thank you.

One has only to take an hour or two to sit at a kitchen table across from any one of these "ordinary" people to hear about life's defining moments—hard times and good; times of laughter, tears, and regrets; tender scenes; turning points; and private victories. Theirs are the unforgettable stories gleaned from nearly a century of living on Earth during this, the dispensation of the fulness of times.

We have had the remarkable experience of interviewing nearly one hundred of these elderly members of our society. When we asked for an interview, their first response was usually "Me? Are you sure you want to interview me?" And then, with a smile and gracious hospitality, they welcomed us into their homes or apartments. Some cringed at the idea of having their picture taken, worrying (even at the age of eighty plus) if the camera will make them "look fat." But, whether they sat in a wheelchair in a rest home or were enjoying the newly built home of their dreams, pictures of family inevitably adorned the walls, and we nearly always detected a sense of peace, gratitude, and acceptance of the things they had learned in this life.

Dorothy Hellberg, now deceased, was a resident for several years in the Sunshine Terrace nursing home in Logan, Utah. She had strong feelings about misconceptions regarding the elderly. While living at the nursing home, this well-educated woman edited a newsletter called ***Terrace Talk.*** In one of her columns, she wrote:

> *Among the hobbies I enjoy, I love working crossword puzzles. The other night I needed a six-letter word meaning "old." It came out "senile" and I was furious! In no way does "old" mean "senile." "Old" means well-worn, minus the rough edges. "Old" is experience. "Old" is tolerance and understanding.*
>
> *Young people, I hope you will listen to us. We who have been on the tree of life for so long love you dearly. In turn, we need your love. We all need each other. Much sooner than you think, you will take our place.*
>
> *Young and old, well and halt, may we all rejoice together in*

sharing our talents and wisdom, thus doing our share in building up God's kingdom here on earth.

We couldn't agree more. Therefore, we invite you to come, sit a spell, and listen to the simple stories of life. This is not Homer's ***Iliad*** with the grandeur of mighty political battles and the dramatic rise and fall of ancient heroes. But rather, it is the story of private battles, quiet victories, and deeply felt emotions. We have come away with our own personal heroes—you'll find them on the following pages. We would never have known the "Mount Everests" they have climbed if we had not taken the time to ask and then listen.

Our deepest hope is that you will be moved as they relive and share life's simple yet profound moments. Perhaps you will then be curious about the elderly person you live by, the lady you see frequently at the store, or the gentleman you see out raking leaves each fall. There are books living in the hearts of these neighbors. Stop and talk. Show an interest. Ask a few questions. Both of you will enjoy the time, and you'll walk away a better person.

Children cherish private time with parents

RAMONA HINCKLEY SULLIVAN

My father, Bryant Hinckley, was the manager of the Deseret Gymnasium. How I loved that gymnasium! You could dance and swim. It had everything a little kid could want to do. My father would take me there in the summer to participate in all the activities. Then, he and I would walk from the gym to our home on 7th South between 8th and 9th East. It was a pretty good walk. I loved that walk with him. He would tell me where everyone lived along the way. He knew everyone, being the president of the stake, and he would tell me all about them. I would dance along, and he would hold my hand all the way home. That is a very special memory of my father—just him and me walking hand-in-hand.

Years later I would look back on those summer evening walks and realize how important it is for children to have private, individual time with their parents.

Ramona experienced a great loss at the age of fourteen when her mother, Ada Bitner Hinckley, died of cancer. Now in her nineties, Ramona still gets teary, remembering how difficult it was to lose her mother at such a young age. Thus, it meant even more to her to have a close, meaningful relationship with her father.

Discipline doesn't have to be physical

CLARK L. PUFFER

As a young man, I once went with a group of guys to a movie in our town, then to drinking beer, and then to a café to sober up before going home. While in the café I got a tap on my shoulder. I looked up, and it was my mother. She said, "Clark, I hope you are proud of yourself tonight," and then she left. That was the worst licking I ever received. It was worse than any physical punishment. I never did those things again.

Clark grew to appreciate how his mother handled certain situations. He also admired his maternal grandmother. When his parents divorced, Clark and his brother and his mother went to live with his grandmother. "She had nothing," he remembers. "She was poor and growing older, and yet she welcomed us into her home. I learned that whatever I have, even if it is very little, I can still share it to help someone else."

Clothes don't have to be expensive, just "in good taste"

RICHARD CUDDY HOWE

My mother was a very refined person. She believed in courtesy, manners, and behaving properly. If I ever did anything she thought was improper, she would always say, "It isn't in very good taste." So I learned that lesson early on. I think about that all the time because today the way people act and dress—the words "good taste" have just gone out of our vocabulary.

My folks always shopped at ZCMI. When we shopped, Mother required me to wear my Sunday-best clothes. She would also wear her best dress, along with a hat and white gloves. On the way home I was already loosening my tie and getting ready to get into my play clothes.

Today, when I go to a nice place to have dinner and see someone coming in wearing Levi's and tennis shoes, I just kind of shake my head and say, "Mother wouldn't approve of that."

When Richard's mother raised him to have respect for how he dressed in public, she unwittingly prepared him for one aspect of his life's work. For more than twenty years, Richard would spend most of his day wearing black judicial robes as he served as a highly respected justice of the Utah Supreme Court. Previous to that appointment, Richard served for twelve years in the Utah House of Representatives, where he became Speaker of the House. He then spent six years in the Utah Senate.

Treat everyone the way you want to be treated

TED S. PERRY

I became a lawyer and practiced law with my father. One of my first cases was an automobile accident. The people were seriously injured, and the other driver was clearly at fault. Our client wanted to recover his money and then some.

My father told me and the client in the office, "We are not the usual kind of lawyers. We will recover your medical expenses and our attorney fees, but we're not going to ask anything for pain or suffering and extra damages." He continued, "We know this man is at fault, but he's a person like you and me. He doesn't have the money."

The client spoke up. "They're insured, aren't they?"

Dad said, "Well, even if they are insured, someone will pay the bill because someone else is negligent. And they really shouldn't have to, should they?"

And I asked, "Dad, how are you going to make money practicing law this way?" But the case was settled, and our clients got their medical expenses and attorney fees paid.

Afterwards, Dad said to me, "Remember, son—before you're a lawyer, you're a Christian. You treat everybody the way you would like to be treated." We were not rich lawyers, but we always got by.

Ted has spent a lot of time in a suit and tie. His wife claims she has ironed a white shirt for him at least once a day for all their married life. Ted had a successful law practice for thirty-six years and was a circuit court judge for eleven years. He served a term as mayor of Logan, Utah, was chairman of the board of trustees of the Logan Regional Hospital, and was director of the First National Bank in Logan.

Sometimes parents have to put on a brave front

BARBARA BRADSHAW SMITH

When my mother was fourteen years old, she stood beside her mother, my grandmother, watching an electrical storm. My grandmother was a doctor. She wore a watch over her heart so she could tell what time a baby was born or a person died, just by checking her watch. Tradition says that watch attracted a lightning bolt. It hit my grandmother and went over and hit my mother. Both of them were very sick. They didn't think my grandmother would live. But they both lived.

My mother, after that, was very afraid of lightning, but she never told us children. When there was a lightning storm, she would squeeze all of us into a closet. We would sit on raincoats, and she would tell us stories until the lightning was over. We never knew she, too, was afraid. It was wonderful to be there with her. She never divulged her great fear until we were much older.

Barbara has seven children, thirty-nine grandchildren, and ninety-one great-grandchildren. She enjoys working at the temple once a week. Her hobbies include collecting pictures for her family history book to eventually be given to her children and grandchildren. She belongs to several church study groups and two social groups. Barbara served as general president of the Relief Society from 1974 to 1984.

We can't replace our loved ones

MELLA PETERSON WILKINSON

When I was in the seventh grade, we were to play a basketball game in Monroe, Utah, which is about thirty-five miles away from where I lived. I volunteered to let our principal, Mr. Overson, drive us in our family car. On our way home, we were singing songs, celebrating our victory at the game, and then suddenly boom! We ran smack into a horse. We stopped, of course, and found out the horse wasn't injured. The car was slightly damaged but not much. I was nervous the rest of the way home, knowing I had to tell my dad.

When I got home, I thought he would be really mad. When I told my dad, he just looked at me for a long time. Then he said, "Was anyone hurt?"

I said, "No."

He was relieved and then said, "We can always replace cars, but we can't replace our loved ones." Then he put his arms around me, and I thought, I have the best dad in the whole wide world.

Mella's father, Conrad Erastus Peterson, mayor of Salinas, Utah, was well-known as "a kind-hearted and charitable man." Mella remembers the love and warmth she felt that night as her dad held her in his arms. It remained a sweet memory with her for the rest of her life.

Mother taught me the fine art of making friends

BETH FRANCIS TITENSOR

Mother never let anyone get by her without being a friend. There was a man in our ward, the ward clerk, who was the worst sourpuss you could ever imagine. He was always frowning. My mother said, "I'm not going to let him get away with that." So she went out of her way to be nice to him. She would take him little favors and ask his advice. It wasn't long before this man just lighted up when she came around. That was one of the best lessons she ever taught me. Now, when someone ignores or rebuffs me, I think of what Mother did, and I say, "You're not going to get away with that. You're going to become my best friend."

Part of having the energy to reach out to others has to do with feeling good and living a healthy lifestyle, Beth says. She attributes her good health to exercise, eating right, and yoga. Beth was the first female cheerleader at Brigham Young University in 1939. Now in her late eighties, she believes you need to "think healthy" and then live to be that way. Beth has seven children, thirteen grandchildren, and seven great-grandchildren. She serves as an ordinance worker in the Logan Utah Temple for Spanish speakers one day a week.

Work hard and be frugal

JESSE JACOB ZOLLINGER

I grew up in the years of the Great Depression. There was a 30 percent unemployment rate then, and jobs were hard to come by. We had very little money and had to be careful in our expenditures.

My mother, God bless her, worked side by side with Father in providing for our needs and paying our bills. I never heard a murmur from her as she did her part in making our home a place where the spirit of the Lord could be felt. Even though we produced carloads of the finest apples, she always felt she had to use those we couldn't sell—the culls—to cook with at home. I haven't forgotten the time when she asked me to find her some cooking apples. I took her some real nice ones. She scolded me and sent me back for some "rejects."

These lessons in frugality contributed much to my success in life. Using an old wood and coal stove, Mother canned and bottled fruit and vegetables all summer long so that our food storage would be well stocked. She made the best bread, pies, and pastries of all kinds. She washed, sewed, ironed, and mended our clothes. She was the most unselfish person I have ever known.

There was, however, one item that Mother prepared that appeared on the dinner table too often, I thought, and that was small, creamed onions. I hated them, but I was encouraged to eat them. I think my parents operated on the assumption that if I ate them I would like them, but it didn't work that way. One day I was served headcheese made from parts of a hog's head. Boy, all of a sudden creamed onions became a delicacy!

Jesse rarely wore anything other than a pair of overalls, unless he was going to church or the temple. When he died, he left three well-worn pairs to be inherited by three lucky descendants. He loved genealogy and treasured a trip to Switzerland to see where his mother was born. He hated going to the doctor and had a famous bit of health advice for his family: "The whiter the bread, the sooner you're dead." He read the scriptures every day and planted a huge garden—including an acre of peas! He and his wife, Idona, were married sixty-seven years and died exactly one month apart.

Enduring pain to save some money

Willis "Bill" McBride

I was constantly playing tricks on my parents. I once put a starfish in their bed. I don't think they ever figured out what it was. And I used to climb on top of our barn and run across the roof when I knew my mother was watching. Then I would stand on one leg just to scare her.

But one time I endured a lot of physical pain just to save them some money.

I got my first pony when I was five years old. I was the most thrilled little boy in the world, even though she was the orneriest, meanest little horse that ever lived. I believe she ditched me a hundred times or more. She bit, kicked, and tromped me. Once, my friend John Wilson and I were riding her when my foot touched her flank. She put her head down and started to buck. She threw both of us, and I landed on the bottom. My friend was on top. This left me with both bones in my lower left arm broken. The break was so bad it looked as if my fingers could touch the elbow on the same arm.

My dad took me in a wagon to Dr. Cutler's. He told Dad the price to set the arm was five dollars cheaper if I didn't have an anesthetic. Five dollars was a lot of money in those days and pain was cheap, so Dad pulled on one end of the arm and the doctor on the other. I could hear the bones grate and grind, as they worked them back in place. After it was over I felt like quite a hero because I had saved my parents five dollars.

Bill's grandchildren could count on two things whenever they went to visit their Grandpa McBride. First, they knew Grandpa would spend time doing something fun with them. Even in the winter, Grandpa would use his horse and a long rope to pull them on an inner tube across the snow. Second, they would always walk out the door to go home with an ice-cream cone in their hand. Every visit.

Sometimes you just have to be tough

RULON FRANCIS THOMPSON

Every summer from the time I was about six years old until I was ten, we had an annual haircutting ritual. When school was out, we went up to "Pack's place." They had some old hand clippers they used to clip the cattle with, and we'd take turns clipping each other's hair. We'd clip it very close. Basically, the rule was when all the hair was gone, you were through.

Oh boy, I can just feel it now! The clippers would cut a few hairs but also pull out quite a few, too. It would just about take you right off your feet every time. If you were strong enough to stand it 'til you got through, you were a pretty good man. We were too big to cry; but it hurt so bad that the tears would just roll; but we'd stand there and endure it. Everybody did it. It would keep you cool in the summer, and you didn't have to comb anything. Besides, you had to have a haircut or they'd call you "chicken," and you didn't want to be that!

I'd go home and Mother would feel so bad she would sometimes cry, but for another reason. With our new haircuts we looked like a bunch of monkeys.

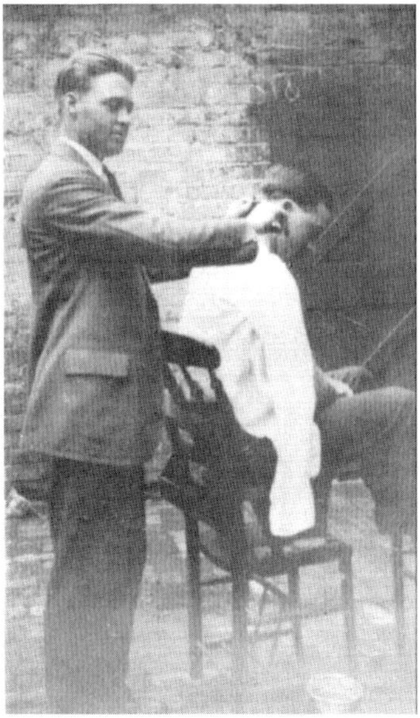

Rulon served a full-time mission to the British Isles where, interestingly enough, he served as the mission barber. He had three mission presidents who became prominent Church leaders: David O. McKay, James E. Talmage, and John A. Widtsoe. He and his wife, Jennie, had been married forty-three years before she died in 1972. He is remembered for his willingness to serve others, to lift them with his kindness and his marvelous sense of humor.

Use your talents to bless the lives of others

Bette Smith Kirk

I spent much of my young adult years in the water. I have enjoyed it even though I've had a few scary moments. When I was twelve, I almost drowned while trying to save my seven-year-old brother. I didn't know how to swim, and I was under water about three minutes. Even though they had to work hard on me, my brother and I were rescued. I decided right then that I was going to learn how to swim, and I was going to be a lifeguard. Finally, after years of waiting, I learned how to swim in the Navy pool at Treasure Island where I worked. Later, in San Francisco, my brother and I took a life saving course. Not only did I attain my goal of learning how to swim and be a lifeguard but I had an added bonus of teaching swimming to nonswimmers.

Many years later, a typhoon struck Guam, where my husband was stationed in the Navy. The waves were so big they were hitting the coconut trees. Parents had left their children on the beach swimming for the afternoon. The storm struck suddenly and without warning. The waves were too high, and the children couldn't get to shore. They were all yelling and screaming. It seemed as if I pulled fifty children out of the water that day.

I still love to swim and to teach anyone who needs help, even though I now spend more time relaxing in the pool watching everybody else having fun.

Bette loves the ocean. She says a perfect day for her would be to sit on a sandy knoll and the closer to the ocean, the better. She loves the smell of seaweed and salt water, hearing the seagulls, and watching the waves coming in and going out. Bette says, "Everywhere I look, I see what the Lord has given us to enjoy!"

I SET OUT A CHILD AND CAME BACK A MAN

LAMONT HARRIS

I had a summer job as a teenager that made me grow up in a hurry. My brother-in-law owned a dry farm in the remote area of Park Valley, Utah, one hundred miles west of where I grew up in Cache Valley. When I was sixteen years old, I was sent to spend the first of two summers there. I have to admit I was scared and afraid. I didn't want to go. I went out to Park Valley all alone with four head of horses and a wagon. I loaded up the wagon with tools, hay, and provisions and set out like a child.

I had never worked on a farm. I had to learn how to do things myself. Nobody taught me. I lived in a tent first and then a log cabin. I used to sit on the roof of that cabin and play my trumpet. You could hear the echo through the valley for miles. Sometimes I went for days and weeks without seeing anyone. I felt so alone I used to cry myself to sleep. But, as I said, the experience made me grow up in a hurry. I may have loaded up the wagon and set out as a child, but I came back a man.

Lamont Harris's first wife died, leaving him with three sons and one daughter to raise. Then his second wife, who was divorced from her first husband, brought two more sons to the family. Together, late in life, they had one daughter. It was a challenge to put food on the table, but Lamont worked at the Amalgamated Sugar Factory for many years and also as a house painter. The house was always filled with laughter and music. Lamont tended a beautiful yard filled with his favorite flowers.

Get in Shape—Run from Evil

J. L. JAUSSI

I started school very young and was smaller than most of my classmates. I had little chance of being outstanding in athletics and other activities. I remember many nights being chased home by a half dozen lads from school. It seemed to be their favorite pastime to annoy and tease me, but through it all I seemed to survive.

Being chased by those boys was probably the very thing that helped me later in life to meet many of the challenges that I have had to face. It could also be one of the reasons I excelled in track at Ricks College, later known as BYU–Idaho, and brought home many awards for running.

For several years J. L. was the district coordinator of seminaries for The Church of Jesus Christ of Latter-day Saints. He started the first seminary and institute programs in the midwestern states, and also in Australia. He enjoys reading Louis L'Amour novels and LDS Church books. He feels that all of his goals or dreams have been met, except one—he always wanted to own a cattle ranch. For now, the novels will have to suffice.

The greatest invention? The can opener!

LAWRENCE CANTWELL

I can remember our first telephone. It had a crank on the side and hung on the wall of our home. I remember, too, our first radio, which we purchased in a Chicago store for $6.70. And I can remember the first television in Smithfield, Utah. The year was 1951. It was black-and-white, and to this day, I like black-and-white television better than color. I think the picture is clearer. However, I feel the greatest invention was the can opener! I kept cutting myself as a kid because all I had to open a can was a knife. I felt that the can opener was the greatest invention ever made, because I was hungry.

Lawrence grew up a loner, roaming the hills on the east side of Smithfield, Utah, on his horse, exploring the mountains. He learned early where all the trails were and gained a great love for nature. He felt more at home in the mountains than he did in town. Most of the food he ate he found in the canyons.

Is this what the Holy Ghost feels like?

COLLEEN HINCKLEY MAXWELL

Although I didn't know it at the time, I was coming down with measles the very day I was baptized. I remember it so clearly. I was baptized in the baptismal font in the Salt Lake Tabernacle on Temple Square in Salt Lake City. But I was so sick I could hardly hold my head up, and I had a fever. I remember wondering, Is this what the Holy Ghost feels like?

Colleen Hinckley Maxwell was born and reared in Salt Lake City and is the widow of Elder Neal A. Maxwell of the Quorum of the Twelve Apostles. Colleen graduated from the University of Utah in homemaking education, which she then taught in an Arizona school. Her family members are still the beneficiaries of her superb sewing and cooking skills. She and her deceased husband have four children and twenty-four grandchildren. She is known as a gracious hostess and an outstanding cook.

Sometimes it's better to keep your mouth shut!

RULON FRANCIS THOMPSON

I was baptized north of Richmond, Utah. The area was all covered with hawthorn bushes and was known as Muddy River. It is now called the Cub River. Several boys were baptized that day. I remember how cold the water was. It took our breath away as we waded out into the river to where we were to be immersed. The water came almost up to our shoulders. When one of the boys came up out of the water, he said, "Hell, that's cold!" He was immediately immersed in the water again. When he came up the second time, he kept his mouth shut.

Rulon (center) was adored by his children and grandchildren. On his eightieth birthday they expressed gratitude for the memories they would always have of the things they did with him: working with him in the garden using miniature yard tools that he had bought for them, deer hunting, berry picking, camping, and hauling hay. He had many friends and was considered a good speaker. When he died, his family noted that he had spoken at 102 funerals.

An unusual place for a baptism

RAMONA HINCKLEY SULLIVAN

My father was the manager of the Deseret Gymnasium in Salt Lake City. My sister Ruth and I were baptized in the swimming pool there. The gym was closed that day, and it was so nice and quiet and pretty much deserted. We even got to swim for a while afterwards. I had a white dress on, and I thought how strange it was to wear a dress into the swimming pool.

Ramona, now in her nineties, was the most athletic of the three daughters born to Bryant and Ada Bitner Hinckley, so perhaps it was fitting that she was baptized in a swimming pool. While raising her family, she loved to play golf, swim, and ride horses, and she enjoyed boating with her husband and children in the West at Lake Powell, Flaming Gorge, and Lake Tahoe.

An unforgettable day at the temple

MELLA PETERSON WILKINSON

The biggest day of my life occurred when I turned eight years old and was now eligible to be baptized. I couldn't sleep the night before. What would it be like? Would I be frightened? After a prayer in the morning, we were on our way to the Manti Temple. Back then it was about a two-hour drive, but it seemed so far. Finally, we drove into Manti on Main Street. As we turned east, there it was, that beautiful Manti Temple. What a breathtaking sight! The marble structure, shining and glistening in the bright sun, sitting on a grassy green hill. As we turned left to go up the hill behind the temple, I could not take my eyes from that marvelous sight. We parked almost in front of the door. As we got out of the car, I held my mom's hand very tight.

I could feel a calming spirit and knew my Heavenly Father was there and was pleased with me. Finally, I was dressed all in white. As we walked to the steps of the font, I was a wee bit frightened. As my father reached for my hand and led me into the water, all my fears left me. I was baptized and confirmed by my father. I was thinking, Now I am really a member of The Church of Jesus Christ of Latter-day Saints.

After we were dressed we walked around the southwest corner of the temple. My grandma Thora Nelson told me that when she was a young girl, she had the honor of placing the Bible, Book of Mormon, Pearl of Great Price, and Doctrine and Covenants in a box and covering it with one of the marble blocks and placing them in the cornerstone. It was sealed as the Manti Temple was being built. It was a very peaceful and thrilling moment as we all felt the Spirit of our Heavenly Father.

We had a guide who led us up the winding stairs to the very top of the west tower of the temple. What a breathtaking sight. We could overlook the whole Sanpete Valley for miles and miles. What an inspiration! What a sight—to look out and see what so many people had sacrificed to build. I was a very tired and excited little girl as we started on our way back home.

Mella was as excited about her baptism as any eight-year-old could be. Another very spiritual event would take place in just a few years. She received her patriarchal blessing from Patriarch Lazenby. His wife took notes by hand, and Mella has that copy. The Lazenbys opened their living room twice a month to give patriarchal blessings. The chairs were all upholstered in velvet. Mella writes in her autobiography, "I sat in one of the chairs, and when Patriarch Lazenby put his hands on my head and started my blessing, I knew the Church was true. I was thirteen."

The Primary sisters loved me as one of their own children

HAVEN J. BARLOW

My mother was killed in an automobile-train accident when I was nine months old. Because I was raised by a stepmother and my father, I always worried about who would take care of me if something happened to them. When I was three or four years old, my father served as a member of the Clearfield town council. I couldn't go to sleep at night when he was away. I used to sit up those nights in my pajamas to watch for his car to come down the street and pull into our driveway. I remember that in Primary, the women were so nice. They were like mothers to me. I came to the conclusion that if something happened, I always had a place with any of those women. It was as if I had a lot of mothers! They convinced me that they loved me as much as they loved their own children. That's a great feeling for a teacher to convey to her students.

Even with a long list of accomplishments in the world of business and government, Haven has one big regret in life: "I worked hard to get my Eagle Scout rank. I got all the hard parts done. I was a Life Scout and only had to pass one easy merit badge called Service in the Community. Then I suddenly lost interest. I have gone through life regretting that ever since, especially when I had to fill out applications for scholarships and achievements. I always thought, Oh! If only I could have said I got my Eagle badge! I wish my parents had put their foot down and said, 'Haven, this is going to be important for you for the rest of your life. You're going to regret this if you don't finish your last merit badge.' I tell all my grandsons, 'Get your Eagle badge, and don't mess it up like I did.'"

You can work, can't you?

TED S. PERRY

The LDS Church Primary organization used to have a birthday pennies fund to donate to the Primary Children's Hospital. On your birthday you were supposed to bring pennies, the number according to your age. Like most families we were poor, and we children just didn't ask for money. I knew my birthday was coming up, and I was too embarrassed to ask for money. So finally I went to my teacher and told her that I wasn't going to be able to give birthday pennies because it took all our money just to keep us fed and clothed.

She said, "You can work, can't you?"

I replied, "Yes."

She said, "I will find you a job so you can earn your birthday pennies."

I went to every teacher in Primary and told them the same story and got a job, usually shoveling snow, because my birthday was in January. That's how I earned my birthday pennies.

Ted served a full-time mission for the Church, having been called to the East Central States Mission. He eventually established a successful law practice for thirty-six years and was a municipal court judge for eleven years. He is a brother to Elder L. Tom Perry of the Quorum of the Twelve Apostles. Ted has served as a patriarch in Logan, Utah, for twenty-two years, a calling he loves. He says the oldest person to whom he has given a patriarchal blessing was ninety-seven years old.

YOUR MOTHER WANTS TO KNOW . . .

BARBARA BRADSHAW SMITH

When my children were young, I made report cards that they took to Primary. I wanted to make sure that they were being good children. The Primary teacher would sign them and send them back to me. One of my children didn't get very good marks. So, that gave me the information I needed to spend more time with this child. Those report cards really did help.

As a young girl, Barbara dreamed of being a mother and having a family. Those dreams came true. Barbara and her husband, Douglas, have seven children, thirty-nine grandchildren, and ninety-one great-grandchildren. Barbara served as the general president of the Relief Society from 1974 through 1984.

We needed to solve a problem

LORRAINE LARSON LARSEN

My favorite Church calling was teaching the Guide Patrol in Primary—the eleven-year-old boys. I had that calling for thirteen and a half years, and I loved every minute of it.

The only boy in all those years that gave me trouble was a young man who has since grown up, served as a mission president, and is the cofounder and CEO of an international manufacturing company. Even as a young boy, he was a leader.

I remember one incident in particular. I had had the same five boys in my Guide Patrol class for nine months. They were a pretty tight-knit group. After several months two new boys who were going to be turning eleven years would be coming into my class. The boys already in my class decided they did not want these two new boys coming in. They said, "They can get another teacher for them." This certain young man, the leader, decided that he was going to make things miserable for me if these two boys came into the class. I would go early and get my classroom all set up and then, after opening exercises in the chapel, we'd go into the classroom and all of my materials would be scattered all over the room, papers torn, pictures ripped—it was awful! I shed a lot of tears.

Finally, I couldn't take it any longer. I sat down in front of the class and said, "You boys are going home. You can't come to the Church house and behave this way. Go home, and I'm going to come visit your parents." They were all good kids; we just needed to solve this problem.

A counselor in the Primary presidency and I went first to see the parents of the ringleader. I was afraid the parents wouldn't believe me when I told them what their son had been doing at Primary. When I got to the house, I asked to speak with both parents and their son. Not only did their son come and join us, but—to my great surprise—he confessed to everything and apologized to me and to his parents. They were shocked. They never would have believed what was happening at Primary, and yet their son confessed.

Now, when I see this man around town, he comes up to me, gives me a hug, and asks, "How's my favorite Primary teacher?!"

After years of service to the young boys in her ward Primary organization, Lorraine now loves spending precious time with her grandchildren. She has one grandson, in particular, who visits her often. Together they play catch with a football or softball, make cookies, and recently climbed a tree together. Lorraine works at the Logan Utah Temple answering the phone, and she serves in a Relief Society presidency.

The word of the Lord can be communicated in many ways

LEONARD JAMES ARRINGTON

I recall a unique activity in the Scouting program I participated in while growing up near Twin Falls, Idaho. As a part of our qualification for First Class, we had to learn how to send and receive semaphore messages, using flags like those that signalmen used on ships. I learned the telegraphic code and could send and receive messages through tapping as well as through flags. One Sunday the bishop turned the sacrament meeting over to the Scouts, and he suggested we show the congregation how to send messages by flags.

After the sacrament portion of the meeting had been completed, I was stationed in the rear of the chapel, and fellow scouter Freddie Babbel was placed on the stand at the pulpit. The bishop secretly gave a message to Freddie, who then sent it to me by flag. From the back of the chapel, I took it down, letter by letter, ran up to the stand, and announced to the astonished congregation that Freddie had just sent me a piece of scripture, a passage from the Book of Mormon. This was a thrill for Freddie and me as well as the congregation. It made us realize the variety of methods mankind has created and perfected to use in communicating with each other.

Leonard (left) learned many ways to communicate important messages. He left the family farm in Idaho to attend college, the first of his siblings to do so. He became a scholar and a professor at Utah State University and Brigham Young University. Eventually he was called by the First Presidency of The Church of Jesus Christ of Latter-day Saints to be the Church historian. By the time he passed away at age eighty-one, he had written twenty-six books and published hundreds of articles. He was a beloved mentor to a whole generation of students of LDS Church history.

Choose a Good Role Model

RAMONA HINCKLEY SULLIVAN

Marjorie Pay, the future wife of President Gordon B. Hinckley, was our neighbor while I was growing up. She taught my Mutual class one year. In one of the classes, she taught us how to be a lady and how to dress. She told us to keep clean and keep our hair washed. She said, "Keep your clothes nice. Keep them pressed. Hang them up every time you come in the house so they're always ready to go. Don't let your clothes just fall on the floor." She was just as cute as pie! It was great. The whole class was absolutely enthralled with this dear woman and her example. You can imagine how happy I was that she became a member of our family when she married my oldest brother, Gordon.

Ramona learned graciousness, cleanliness, and an appreciation for artistic things from people around her whom she admired. She put these talents to good use. Ramona attended the Art Institute of Chicago while the Hinckley family lived nearby and her father, Bryant, served as mission president in that area. She later graduated from Brigham Young University with a degree in art. She has often used a technique to add color to black-and-white photographs. Ramona enjoys other artistic projects as well.

Important people can be nice, too

RICHARD CUDDY HOWE

I grew up thinking that "important" people were really too busy to be nice. But throughout the years when I was involved a lot in politics, I found that was not true. Some of the most gracious people I have met have been individuals who were considered famous or "important" people. There are exceptions, of course.

Hubert Humphrey, a senator from Minnesota and then vice president of the United States, visited us in Utah in 1960. We traveled with his group around the area and ended up in Cache Valley to visit the one or two Democrats there. We ended up all in one car because others in the group had dropped out. It was in the winter, and I had left my car in Brigham City. On the way back to my car, I said to the driver, "Why don't you wait a few minutes to see if my car will start?" It was close to midnight, and it was storming. I got into my car, and it didn't start. The next thing I knew Hubert Humphrey was at my window saying, "Dick, release the hood." He continued, "I have one of these Fords. When they don't start, you have to stick your finger in the choke and open it up." Well, he did just that, and the car started right up. Such experiences convinced me that famous people can be very gracious.

Richard had many opportunities to rub shoulders with well-known and highly successful people, especially in politics and in the legal system. He served for twelve years in the Utah House of Representatives, six years in the Utah Senate, and was appointed a justice of the Utah Supreme Court. He is the only person in Utah history to have served as a member of all three of those legislative and judicial bodies.

A Scout camp that resulted in a career decision

D. PETER LASSIG, SR.

I am often asked, "How does a person end up as the head gardener at Temple Square?" As I look back, there was a series of events that eventually put me in the right place at the right time.

When I was a Boy Scout, twelve years old, our Scoutmaster took us up to Camp Steiner for summer camp. The first morning we were to go on a nature trail, where we would learn about twelve flowers. We got to the first flower, and they named it. At that moment my heart just thumped. I couldn't believe how excited I was. After the Scout leader named the second and the third flower, I thought, This is it! This is my life. This is where I want to be! This is what I want to do!

A few years later, in high school, I took a horticulture class from an outstanding teacher. After a few classes, he told me I needed to commit my life to horticulture, and I knew he was absolutely right.

And finally, years ago, some time prior to October conference, I was walking around Temple Square with my father. I was eighteen years old. We went to see the head gardener, Irvin T. Nelson, in his office. I knocked on the door and asked if we could chat. After a few moments of conversation, my father (who was a brusque German) said, "Peter, why don't you tell him what you're really here for?"

I stammered and stuttered.

Then my father said, "He's here because he wants your job."

Brother Nelson turned to me and said, "Is that true?"

And I said, "Well, yes . . . yes, but you can stay as long as you want."

Before the year was out, he had hired me. I worked for him for about sixteen years as an apprentice. When he retired, I took over his position and worked as head gardener at Temple Square for the next thirty-one years. I have never had any regrets.

Peter spent much of his life with his hands in the soil, planting and nurturing that which literally millions of others would enjoy. He received a degree in ornamental horticulture and a minor in field botany from Brigham Young University. He also completed three years of graduate studies in landscape architecture at Utah State University. He was an apprentice at LDS Church headquarters in their flower gardens for sixteen years. He then served as manager of Grounds Services at Church headquarters from 1972 until he retired. He didn't particularly like the official title of the position he held all those years. He much preferred to be known simply as "head gardener."

HITCH YOUR WAGON TO A STAR

VELOY BEYLE BUCKINGHAM

I was bound, bent, and determined that I was not going to remain living in my hometown of Malta, Idaho. I was not going to marry some farmer and be a windblown, dried-up, old farm wife. My eighth grade teacher encouraged me to hitch my wagon to a star and it would lead me towards lofty goals. This inspired me to set some higher goals.

My first dream was to go to college. I was even more determined to do that when one of the men in town told my father that I would never finish school, that I would just get married and quit. That really fired my determination to succeed and graduate.

My high school superintendent, Leslie Sudweeks, knew of my desire to go to college. He also knew that my parents could not afford to send me to school with seven younger ones to take care of and provide for. His brother, Joseph Sudweeks, was a professor at Brigham Young University. Superintendent Sudweeks made arrangements for me to live with his family and work for my room and board.

Traveling to BYU, I rode to Salt Lake City with conference visitors and then took the Bamberger train to Provo, arriving in the late evening. I had never used a telephone, so the stationmaster called the Sudweeks's home. Only the son, David, was home. He was fourteen. He rode his bicycle to the station and put my suitcase on the seat. We walked to his home.

My dear grandmother sent me twenty dollars for books, and I was launched into my freshman year. I went to see someone about employment so I could pay my tuition. I was given a job in the book bindery at Brigham Young University. Sometimes I babysat for twenty-five cents a night. I later transferred to Utah State Agricultural College (now Utah State University) in Logan. I graduated in June 1940.

I will always remember my eighth grade teacher, who encouraged me to hitch my wagon to a star, and I will always be grateful for others who also helped with this journey.

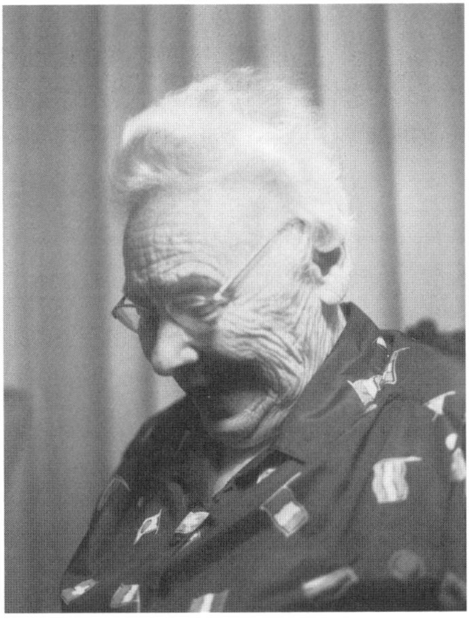

Veloy met her future husband at the University of Idaho in Moscow, Idaho, where she was earning her teaching certificate for the state of Idaho. He had just finished a four-year stretch in the Navy after high school before going to the university. After dating during the summer of 1940, they were married in the Salt Lake Temple. They have two sons.

Everyone needs a good example to follow

COLLEEN HINCKLEY MAXWELL

I had to follow Sister Camilla Kimball as the Spiritual Living teacher in Relief Society in our ward. That was a challenge. Sister Kimball was the first one I was aware of to suggest that the sisters bring their scriptures to Relief Society. She challenged us to read the scriptural assignments for the year, and if we completed them, she would have a luncheon for us at her home. I feel she was ahead of her time in promoting scripture reading in Relief Society. I followed in her footsteps in that calling, and she was always so supportive of me. It was a wonderful calling to receive, because it required so much study and reading of the scriptures to then feel prepared to teach the lesson. I'm so grateful to have had that opportunity to prepare those lessons.

Neal and I have tried, as many other Latter-day Saint families have tried, to provide opportunities for our children and our grandchildren to grow up with a love for the scriptures. We regularly studied the scriptures with our children and later with our grandchildren, as they came along.

Nowadays, young people carry their scriptures around with them when they are barely old enough to walk. One day Neal and I stopped by our daughter's home for a few minutes. She called upstairs to her little four-year-old son, who was napping. "Come quickly. Grandma and Grandpa are here." A sleepy little voice replied, "Should I bring my scriptures?"

Colleen Hinckley married Neal A. Maxwell on November 22, 1950. She is known for the community service she gives and for quietly going about doing good things for her extended family and her neighbors. She loves beauty wherever it can be found—whether in nature, art, literature, or music. Before a recent injury and joint replacement surgery, Colleen loved to play tennis and ride her bike.

A TEACHER CAN TRULY CHANGE YOUR LIFE

HAVEN J. BARLOW

I had a debate coach, Charlie Gardner, who literally changed my life. He instilled a keen desire on my part to look at state and national issues and then debate on those, learning to take a position on either side. One time I'd be in favor, another time against. I learned how to prepare facts and how to prepare for opponents' rebuttal.

My debate coach gave me an interest in public service by giving me a chance to debate public issues. Later, my desire for public service led to an interesting twist of fate. When I first ran for a seat in the Utah State House of Representatives from Davis County, Utah, my opponent was my former debate coach! He was the incumbent. I defeated him, and yet he was very gracious about it.

Haven is the president of Barlow Corporation. He has been involved in real estate and insurance for more than five decades. He is a former president of the Ogden board of realtors. He was a Utah state legislator for forty-two years, six of them as president of the senate. He served in the legislature longer than anyone else in the history of the state of Utah.

Look for a "good" marriage partner

HELEN QUIST MILLIGAN

In choosing a mate, don't pick the tallest and most handsome or the most beautiful. Don't choose one just because that person raises your physical passions. Look for the person who is good from within, the one with substance and worth. And when children come along, play with them! Hold them in your arms and tell them you love them.

Before they passed away, Helen Milligan and her husband, Cleve, had six children, twenty-four grandchildren, and forty-two great-grandchildren. In Helen's last years, her family says, she never complained. She made the best of her situation and would always think of something positive to say. She loved doing family history work, and, on her good days, raising flowers and gardening. On many a summer day, Helen and Cleve could be seen walking hand-in-hand in their neighborhood in Smithfield, Utah.

Make it a matter of prayer

RICHARD CUDDY HOWE

When I was a teenager, our bishop told us that choosing a mate was one of the biggest decisions of our lives. He said, "You boys ought to pray about it." That struck me as being very odd. I thought that you chose your mate by finding someone you fell in love with. However, when I felt I had met the right person, I did as he advised. I made it a matter of prayer. Now, after fity-six years of marriage, I can say that was excellent advice. There is absolutely no question that I married the right young lady.

As a man whose career in law and politics required him to make decisions that would affect the lives of many people, Richard was grateful he chose wisely when he married Juanita Lyon. They are the parents of three sons and three daughters. Richard is the only person in Utah history to have served as a member of the State House of Representatives, the State Senate, and the State Supreme Court.

More than one right way to do things

MARILYN BEE JAUSSI

When a young couple disagrees on something, it doesn't mean that they don't like each other anymore. Each person has a right to their own thoughts. There are compromises, and there is more than one right way to do things. Sometimes it takes a long time to learn this lesson.

Marilyn speaks from experience when she talks about how to improve marriage relationships. She and her husband, J. L., have been married more than sixty-five years. They have five children and twenty-five grandchildren. Marilyn grew up in Georgetown, Idaho. She spends her days reading, exercising, gardening, and doing artwork.

Learn to pay your own way, right from the beginning

EVA FAY ISRAELSEN ANDERSON

On the night before my wedding day, my dad said he had to get the hay into the barn the next morning and he didn't know if he could make it to the wedding. But I knew he was just kidding. They got up really early and got the hay in. We all made it in time to the Logan Temple. Daddy said my husband and I could borrow his car to go on our honeymoon to Yellowstone.

We headed through Logan Canyon and up toward Jackson Hole. Suddenly, as we were driving along, the axle broke on the car and a wheel went running down the road. We sat there in the car—we both were scared and didn't know what to do. Luckily, a forest ranger came by and said, "Well, you can sleep here until morning, and I will put flares around you." There was nothing else we could do, but we heard bears all night. We just sat there and talked all night.

The next morning the ranger called a guy in Jackson to come and get us. It cost us fifty dollars, and that's all the money we had. He had to send to Salt Lake City for a part to repair our car. He let us stay with him the first night, and the next day we went to church and asked the bishop if he had any work we could do. He knew of a farmer and his wife who needed help. For three weeks we worked for them to earn money. We slept in the attic of their house. We called my father and he said he would send us money, but my husband declined the offer. He said, "We will work it off."

Eva Fay and her husband, Nathan, have been married sixty years. In 1994 they sold the family home and built their "dream home"—a wonderful log home on four acres of land she inherited from her father. "It's the joy of life," Eva Fay says with a big smile. "We feel like we're on vacation every day." She designed the home from top to bottom and had it built by a company from Montana. "We had fifty-five people here just the other night, and everybody had a great time," she says. She fills the home with fun and laughter and the enticing aroma of homemade bread.

The key is to "marry well"

Helen Quist Milligan

Cleve and I dated for about six months and were married July 30, 1937, in the Logan temple. We were going to spend our first night in the old Boy Scout cabin in Smithfield Canyon that Cleve had helped build as a young Scout. But when we arrived, the door was open. The cows had been in there, and the place was filled with manure. Then, it started to rain. We spent our first honeymoon night in the car!

After that we had a great time during the summer traveling over Forest Service roads in southern Idaho, living out of a half-ton pickup truck, sleeping under the stars, and stopping at small towns wherever possible. I remember Cleve saying the key to a happy marriage is to "marry well." We never had a major fight all those many years together. Sometimes I think that bothered his Irish blood.

While most of their neighbors were still sleeping or just stirring from their beds, Helen and Cleve were out walking, sometimes holding hands and sometimes carrying a garbage sack between them for litter they often found along the way. They were married for forty-seven years before Cleve passed away. "Daily walks helped us weather the passing years," said Helen. "That's the only time we had to talk things over." They walked one to three miles each day for more than thirteen years.

Buy a cheap meal and then you can buy onions

MELLA PETERSON WILKINSON

There was no "wedding" as such. I was living with my grandmother, and there was no one to give me a nice gathering for a wedding. Clynn, my husband-to-be, and I drove to Ely, Nevada. We got there just as the courthouse was closing. The clerk called in his wife and another person to be the witnesses, and he performed our marriage ceremony. We asked him how much we owed him. He said, "Oh, just name your first child after me."

Then we went out to a restaurant. My husband, who is such an outgoing person, said, "We just got married, and we want the best meal you've got in the house for twenty-five cents." We got the meal for twenty-five cents—and cake with ice cream on top. I was so embarrassed that I was never going to speak to him again. That didn't last long.

On our way back, we stopped in Salt Lake City. We had fifty dollars, so we bought twenty-five pounds of onions, twenty-five pounds of carrots, and twenty-five pounds of potatoes. That was the honeymoon. Later, on May 31, 1939, we were sealed for time and all eternity in the Manti Utah Temple.

While newly married, Clynn wanted to have the family over for Christmas dinner. Mella insisted they didn't have enough money. Clynn took five dollars and bought hamburger, beans, onions, and tomatoes. They served chili, and a family tradition was born. Chili continues to be the main course for Christmas dinner every year for the extended family.

The day was simple, and the marriage endures

ROSETTA THOMPSON WITTORF

I grew up with three older brothers. My brother Bobby had a best friend named Sydney Wittorf. They used to heckle me something fierce. But along about the time that I was nine years old and they were twelve, Sydney asked me to marry him. Well, I guess he meant it because on August 23, 1937, we did just that!

There was no money, and so the day was simple. I wore a white suit that I had sewn myself two years before. But I did get a beautiful, single gardenia corsage and a new pair of white shoes. And oh, I was so proud of those shoes. I wore a size two shoe, so it was difficult to find shoes that fit and even more difficult to afford them. To this day I remember how special I felt. I have learned that it is always important to remember to be happy about what you have and not focus on what you don't have. And that is what I taught our children.

Rosetta and her husband, Sydney, live in southern California and have celebrated their seventieth wedding anniversary. Every Friday, Sydney goes to the store and hand picks a dozen roses for Rosetta. They enjoy watching University of Southern California football on television and getting together with their family. They have two daughters and four granddaughters.

A busy wedding day

SARAH "SADIE" BEEBE ELDER

Our wedding date was March 1, 1923. Manti, Utah, was about one hundred miles from Junction, Utah, where we would live—a long trip by horse and wagon! When we stopped for the night, we found that our suitcases had bounced off the wagon and were lost. My sisters had carefully knotted or sewed together all the openings of our nightclothes, but that prank was lost with the suitcases.

As we drove through Marysvale, Utah, we saw a sign "Furniture for Sale." My husband had managed to save two hundred dollars, and with that money we bought used but good quality furniture. If you can imagine it, we got a round oak table and seven oak chairs with leather seats, a beautiful buffet mirror, a brass bed with springs and mattress plus some bedding, a mahogany dresser with oval mirror and matching highboy, and also some dishes and cooking utensils, AND we still had a few dollars left! These would help us start our new life together in Junction.

Sadie and her husband, who was known as Q, were married for nearly fifty-seven years before he died. After his funeral Sadie wasn't left alone to cope. She said, "Two of my daughters stayed with me. One of them stayed two weeks. We went through Q's personal effects and stored them. It was so good to have my daughter with me for those weeks. We slept in the big bed together. We would laugh and talk about all the good memories and experiences we've had as a family. Sometimes one of us would even wake up in the middle of the night remembering some special experience to share."

Trials can turn out to be some of our greatest blessings

GRETCHEN BERLEW

I was very unhappy in my marriage. I had a son, Jerry. My baby girl, Shirley, had died at seven months. I had decided to get a divorce when I discovered I was pregnant again. I thought, "Oh, no! How will I get through this?" I cried and cried. I thought it was the worst thing that could happen to me.

When it was time to deliver the baby, much to my surprise, I had twins—a boy and a girl! I felt so overwhelmed. Even though Tom and Sandy were beautiful, I thought I could not handle two babies alone. I stayed in the marriage for several more years and finally got brave enough to go out on my own.

Now I am in my nineties. I have outlived my oldest son, Jerry, who died of cancer. It is Tom and Sandy who keep me going. We love our time together. They have given me grandchildren and great-grandchildren. How much emptier my old age would be without them! What seemed at the time to be an overwhelming obstacle turned out to be the greatest blessing. I just had to wait it out to realize it.

In her earlier years, every summer Gretchen used to swim across Port Lake, in Michigan, a distance of one and a half miles. She once saved a woman from drowning. While still in high school, she taught ballet and dancing in the family home. On her eightieth birthday she went on a hot air balloon ride. Advice for today's youth? "First, get an education. Second, keep your pride and honor. Third, be very careful—don't mistake passion for love."

God doesn't make mistakes

MARILYN EAMES BAKER

I lost my only daughter when she was twenty-seven years old. She had microcephaly, a neurological disease that affects the entire body. She was bedridden from birth.

We were told she wouldn't live very long, but she lived to be twenty-seven years old. She was like a three-month-old baby in her capabilities, and she never could speak. We fed her with a baby bottle.

You know, I enjoyed the journey. I tried to put it in the perspective of how long she would like to live in that particular body. I knew she was a pure and good spirit who had to go through this refiner's fire. It gave me hope to look at our Savior at this time. He was perfect, yet He had to go through so much suffering. It was difficult at times, but when I walked into our daughter's room, I could feel her spirit. It was like walking into a little bit of heaven.

Would I do this all again? Oh, yes! I believe these special spirits are sent into homes where they will be accepted, homes where their needs would be met. I've learned to have patience and empathy for families who are in these situations. I look at people who are handicapped and feel love and compassion. God doesn't make mistakes. I feel like my daughter reached the full stage of her progression on this earth and then left us. When we pass through the veil, she will be there to greet us.

Marilyn has been married to her beloved David for fifty-five years. "He is still, to this day," she says earnestly, "my best friend, and I still get excited when he comes home." They have six children, five boys and one girl. Their extended family includes ten grandchildren and five great-grandchildren. Marilyn's most deeply felt dreams have been fulfilled. Her advice to young people is: "Stay close to the Lord. Get an education and be kind. In this hurry-up society we tend to get self-centered and self-consumed, not realizing that at times we can be unkind. We're in such a hurry in this moment we call 'life.' Everyone deserves kindness. And furthermore, don't avoid older people! They have a lot to offer and great experiences to share."

There is power in a priesthood blessing

VELOY BEYLE BUCKINGHAM

After my husband came home from World War II, we wanted to have a second child. Our first child was a three-year-old boy, and we didn't want him to grow up by himself. We weren't having much success, but finally I got pregnant.

About three months into the pregnancy, I began to have problems. I never felt life with this child. I never felt it move. The only way the doctor knew the baby was alive was through the heartbeat.

During the pregnancy I was so sick that the doctor put me in the hospital. He came into my hospital room with another doctor. They both tried to find a heartbeat and could not. My doctor told me he was very doubtful about the survival of this child.

After the doctor left, my husband came back with our bishop and his counselor to administer to me. I listened carefully to their prayer. They didn't promise me anything except that the outcome would be the Lord's will. Later on in the night, I felt that first quiver of life.

The next morning when the doctor came in, I knew he would be very surprised at what he would find. He put his stethoscope on me and listened and immediately heard a heartbeat. He ran to the doorway and yelled down the hall, "It's alive! It's alive!"

He came back into the room and asked how that happened. I replied, "My husband came with the bishop and counselor last night, and they administered to me." That prayer brought life into my child.

I had prayed many times myself and told Heavenly Father that if he would let this child live, I would dedicate the child to him. The doctor took him caesarean, and he grew up to be a healthy man.

Veloy met her husband, Don, in Moscow, Idaho, where she was earning her teaching certificate for the state of Idaho. Veloy and Don dated during the summer of 1940 and were married in the Salt Lake Temple. After briefly living near Anchorage, Alaska, her husband was called into active duty in the Navy, serving with the Navy Seabees in Guam. They didn't see each other for several years. They have two sons.

Am I worthy of you?

MARION G. AND IDA JENSEN ROMNEY
AS TOLD BY D. PETER LASSIG, SR.

I was the gardener for Marion G. Romney and his wife, Ida. During those days when I worked on their yard, Ida would often visit with me.

One day Ida came out and said, "Peter, I've had a wonderful experience." She continued, "I've been suffering for many years, worrying that I didn't have anything to offer President Romney. When we married I was a schoolteacher, and I felt I was making a contribution. But as time went by, President Romney became so busy and he needed someone to take care of the house. So I just took care of him while he did his wonderful things.

"As time went by and I saw how much his secretaries admired him and other people admired him, I began to wonder about my place at his side and in the eternities. The more I thought about it, the more agonized I became. I made it a matter of prayer and fasting. And it came to me that I should make an appointment to see him in his office. I made the appointment, but he was very curious, saying, 'You can visit with me anytime you want, Ida.'

"I replied, 'No, I want to visit you in your office.'"

At the appointed time she got all dressed up for the appointment and went in. He was very perplexed. He held the door for her, and she sat down across the desk from him, like most visitors. She said, "You know, Marion, all these years all I have done is take care of you and the family. I've never been a Relief Society president. I've never been a Primary president. I've never been a Young Women's president. I've never held any stake positions. All I've done is take care of you and the children. And as we come to the end of our lives, I don't know if I am worthy of living with you in the eternities."

He got right up from his desk and went around to her side. He gathered her up into his arms and said, "Ida, Ida, I'm in my position because I'm a good executive. I've always wondered if I would be qualified to be your husband in the eternities."

They both shed tears of gratitude, having a deeper love and an even greater appreciation for each other.

Marion G. Romney and Ida Jensen met at Ricks College (now BYU–Idaho) in Rexburg, Idaho, when Marion's father was president of the college and Ida was teaching English. They celebrated fifty-five years together before she passed away in 1979. He served as a member of the Quorum of Twelve Apostles and was a counselor in the First Presidency under two presidents, Harold B. Lee and Spencer W. Kimball. Marion once said that the greatest compliment he ever received was to read Ida's patriarchal blessing and see that she was promised that she would marry someone who was "her equal."

Learn and Work for the Sheer Joy of It

IRENE MAY WOOTEN BATES

When I lived in England, I was very busy with my Church callings. I had three or four callings, and my husband was stake president. Then we moved to Salt Lake City. There were so many people to do the Church work, I didn't have nearly as much to do.

One day my daughter, Linda, came home and saw me watching a soap opera. She said, "Enough of that!" She sent in an application for me to go to the University of Utah. I agreed to do it, and I was in heaven! I found then that a woman has to have self-confidence. I was hungry for intellectual stimulus. I had left school at age fourteen in England. When I went to college, I did it for the intrinsic joy of it. I told my daughter that she had given me a new birth.

Irene was born in Manchester, England, in 1921. She is fascinated by Mormon history and has written and published on different aspects of the history of The Church of Jesus Christ of Latter-day Saints. She and coauthor E. Gary Smith won the Mormon History Association Best Book Award in 1996 for Lost Legacy: The Mormon Office of Presiding Patriarch, *University of Illinois Press, 1996. She and her husband live in Pacific Palisades, California.*

Everyone deserves a second chance

JESSE JACOB ZOLLINGER

It was late one night when the doorbell rang. I wondered who would be calling at this hour of the night. When I opened the door, I was surprised to see Norman Leonhardt, sheriff of Providence City, Utah, standing on the doorstep. He had with him two sad-looking young men who, he said, were university students. He then proceeded to tell me of an interesting event that had just occurred. "These two young men had driven their station wagon onto your property and loaded up some of your pumpkins. While backing out, they ran into a ditch. About this time," continued the sheriff, "I happened along, stopped to give assistance, and noticed the pumpkins in the back of their car. When I asked them where they had gotten them, they admitted taking them out of your field. Now," said the sheriff, "what are you going to do? Do you want to press charges?"

I hesitated and then walked over to their car to view the evidence. I said, "Yes, they need to pay for these pumpkins." I then figured that their bill would come to six dollars. When they couldn't come up with the money, they asked if they could do some work for me to pay the bill. I said that would be OK. We were busy in the apple harvest and could use some extra help. They agreed to come the next Monday morning, which they did. That day they picked until the both of them had earned twelve dollars, which was double what we had previously agreed upon.

Before they left I asked them if they would like to work for me to earn some money for themselves. They liked that suggestion and agreed to come back the next day. When they reported for work, I made it a point to work alongside them because I was impressed with their behavior and good work. One of them was from New York and the other was from another eastern state. They told me they planned to return to their homes when they had sufficient to pay their way. While we worked together, they asked me about the Church. I was glad to answer their questions and explain to them some of our beliefs.

When I paid them, they said, "We are glad we were caught. This experience has taught us a good lesson." We parted good friends.

Jesse established a successful fifty-acre fruit farm in River Heights, Utah. He raised apples, raspberries, blackcaps (black raspberries), and pears. In addition to the fruit, Jesse raised flowers, chickens, and pigs. People came from far and wide every fall to buy his apple cider. In the 1940s the Logan Tenth Ward ordered two barrels of Zollinger cider for a ward party. They set the two barrels on the stage inside the church house. Apparently, the cider had gone "hard," and during the party, one of the barrels exploded, spewing cider all over the stage and soaking the curtains. It was the most memorable ward party anyone there had ever attended.

Share your God-given talents

LAMONT HARRIS

I was known as "the nightingale" in my hometown, Hyde Park, Utah, when I was a little boy. I sang for the silent movies for $1.50 a song, three nights a week, in an old opera house. There used to be a 5:20 P.M. train that came into Smithfield from Ogden, Utah. When the train arrived, they would drop off two tin boxes containing the movies and the music for two songs. I would learn the words and music by 6:20 P.M. Then, under the spotlight, I would sing the songs for the silent pictures.

In addition to that, I remember one Fourth of July when I was five years old. The announcer at our community program called out my name to sing. Mother looked all over for me but couldn't find me anywhere. Finally, I walked up the aisle. Mother looked at me and was surprised at my appearance. She said, "Where did you wash your face?" I replied, "In the ditch." I had parted and patted my hair down with the ditch water and all that goes with it. I was dressed in a homemade outfit made from some old pants. I was lifted up on a stool, and I sang my heart out. The local ladies made sure I got plenty of ice cream and cake after I sang.

My mother taught me that when you have a God-given talent, you should share it, even if it is for just cake and ice cream.

Lamont Harris had a full head of thick black hair, even into his nineties. He was proud to be a descendant of the pioneers who settled Hyde Park, Utah. To the end of his life, he could tell a good story or recite a poem. And his glorious singing voice stayed with him to the end, along with his fun way of playing the piano. He died at the age of ninety-three.

Greatest knowledge comes from doing, not just hearing

ANN ENGLAND BARKER

Early in my life I wrestled with the traditional roles women play. Sometimes I felt I had to be the transitional woman, choosing between what was expected and the options made available to women today. Sometimes I felt I had dreams of my own and that I could not live in the shadow of my husband's successes. I had dreams of my own that needed to be realized.

But I have learned that no fleeting applause can compare with the joys of raising a good family. The greatest satisfaction comes from doing for a family and not just hearing about it. I have gained a great education through raising a family.

Through interacting with and teaching and learning from my husband and children, I have gained things I could never have learned from a textbook, things like patience, love, unselfishness, and strength of character. We all have faults. We all need to have patience, love, and unselfishness for others in our family. Perhaps wedding vows will one day be changed from "love, honor, and obey" to "love, honor, and forgive."

Ann Barker has lived in Smithfield, Utah, for thirty-eight years. She has five children—four girls and one boy—twelve grandchildren, and one great-grandchild. She received a degree in human development and family relations at BYU and graduated from the Logan Institute of Religion on the Utah State University campus. Being a stay-at-home mom has been challenging but rewarding. "I've used that degree in human development every day of my life," she says. Ann especially loves doing family history. She has presented a family history book to each of her children and eventually will have a book for her grandchildren. Another hobby is raising college grandchildren who like to live with her, often for long periods of time.

Prayers are often answered through other people

Peggy Christensen Brewer Holliday

Late one evening just before Christmas I received a devastating phone call. My daughter had been in a very serious car accident in Hawaii. The doctor caring for her said I needed to get there as soon as possible. I hung up the phone wondering, How do I do this? I was a single parent, teaching school. What little money I had I had spent on Christmas presents for my family. I didn't own a credit card.

I walked across the street and told my dear friends what had happened. The husband was a doctor, and he immediately called the physician in Hawaii for more information. His wife called and booked an airline reservation for me to go to Hawaii. She said, "This is our Christmas gift to you. You have a flight leaving tomorrow morning from the Salt Lake airport."

Two of my sons gave me a blessing. The next morning I was on the plane, not knowing where I would stay or how to get around. During a stopover in San Diego, new passengers boarded the plane. I noticed a beautiful woman walking down the aisle. I thought, Oh please don't sit by me. I felt intimidated by this beautiful woman. Of course, she sat by me. She was young and vivacious, a delightful lady. We began to visit. She told me she had been on a business trip and was returning to her home in Hawaii. Then she inquired why I was going to Hawaii. I explained my situation, and she asked, "Which hospital is your daughter in?"

I told her, and she replied, "I live right by that hospital. It is quite a ways away from the airport. How are you getting to the hospital?"

I replied, "I don't know."

She said, "My driver is picking me up, and we'll take you to the hospital."

I bowed my head and said, "Thank you, Heavenly Father."

She then asked, "There aren't any motels out there. Where are you going to stay?"

I again said, "I don't know."

She replied, "You'll stay with me as long as you need to. I have an extra room in my condominium."

Her third question was, "Do you have a way to and from the hospital?" I shook my head and said no, to which she replied, "You can use one of my cars."

This dear woman gave me keys to her house and her car. I stayed with her for eight weeks while I watched and cared for my daughter. This kind woman on the plane was a true angel. I know it was no accident that she and I sat together on that plane. "Thank you, Heavenly Father."

When Peggy boarded the plane to fly to Hawaii to help her daugher, she was no stranger to traveling. Peggy's first husband, Ivan Brewer, worked for the Church Educational System, which afforded them wonderful opportunities to travel to such places as New Zealand, Israel, Jordan, Italy and Germany. They had five children. After Ivan's death in 1984, Peggy taught elementary school in the Davis School District (Utah) for fifteen years to support her children.

The Power of Humble but Earnest Prayer

D. PETER LASSIG, SR.

I had a pituitary disease when I was young. I stopped growing when I was twelve. I had prayed about this particular problem from the age of twelve to the age of twenty-seven. Through the eyes of people I met on my first mission, I can describe what this disease was like. We would knock on the door, and sometimes a little girl or boy would answer the door. Very often, the child would run to his mother and say, "Mother, a man and a little boy are here to see you." I also didn't shave at all until after I turned twenty-seven. Such were the effects of the disease.

When I was set apart for my second mission, a labor mission, a member of the First Council of the Seventy, Levi Edgar Young, gave me the blessing. He was a very small man himself. I told him that I was the oldest of eight children. My brothers were 6′ to 6′ 5″ and my sisters were all about 5′ 11." I said to him, "As you set me apart, I would like you to bless me that I will grow up. The doctors told me I would never have any children and that I would not develop physically."

He placed his hands on my head and said, "I do not bless you that you will grow tall but that you will develop normally."'

In the next six months, I grew from a boy to a man, physically and spiritually, no more high voice or lack of hair. At the time of the blessing, I was 5′ 2″ and grew to be 5′ 7″.

Peter Lassig believes one of the greatest dreams in his life has been realized, that of having children who love him, honor him, and love to be around him. Another dream came true when he was able to design and build a beautiful home in Salt Lake City. But his greatest dream, his highest hope, came true when his eldest son announced he had decided to go on a full-time LDS mission. For Peter, it was an unexpected and sweet spiritual experience to hear of his son's new plans. Because of this son's decision and example, five other Lassig children have also served as missionaries.

"Blank Page" Prayer

Crawford Gates

I began composing music at the age of eight, soon after my baptism. Before I started the process of composing, I would kneel by the piano and offer a prayer. I would ask the Lord to give me inspiration and bless my work. This has always been a part of my life. As a young man, I heard a talk in church that taught that when we receive the gift of the Holy Ghost, we receive additional special gifts. I discovered at an early age that music was my special gift.

I offered two kinds of prayers. One kind I called the "blank page prayer." In this prayer I asked the Lord to inspire me to know what to put on my blank pages. Then there were times when I would have a beautiful experience, where I would have wonderful things come to my mind. I would write them down, and it would take two to four pages, maybe more. This second kind of prayer I called the "full page prayer of thanks." It was just that—a prayer in which I thanked the Lord for helping me.

Crawford Gates, often referred to as the trailblazer for today's Mormon media composers, has created 854 arrangements and compositions, many of which are sacred and religious in nature. He composed the music to "Our Savior's Love," which can be found in the 1985 LDS Church hymnal.

Prayer can help you find your way

PEGGY CHRISTENSEN BREWER HOLLIDAY

It was the winter of 1984, and Ivan, my husband, was in a hospital in Salt Lake City, dying of leukemia. It was so foggy. For a time there were weeks when we didn't see the sun. I spent many hours, perhaps hundreds of hours, sitting with my husband. Periodically, I would leave the hospital and go home to catch up on things.

One night I decided I would drive home and return the next day. When I got into the car, the fog was so dense I could hardly see. As I looked out across the valley, there was absolutely no valley to see. Not a single light could be seen. As I made a couple of turns, I realized I was completely lost. I knew I was still in the parking lot at the university of Utah, but I had no point of reference. I didn't know where I was or how to get back on the road that led to our home. It was one of those few times when I felt totally and completely discouraged.

I remember I bowed my head in the car and wept bitter tears. I said to my Heavenly Father, "How can I raise my family and teach them all the things they need to know and provide for them physically and spiritually when I can't even find my way home?" I poured out my heart to my Heavenly Father.

Then I raised my head and eyes. For just a moment, the briefest moment, the fog lifted just enough for me to see the dome of the Utah State Capital building. It gave me a point of reference. I was then able to maneuver myself back onto the road and make my way to the freeway. As soon as I was safely on my way home, the fog closed in again.

Peggy grew up in Hooper, Utah. She has five children, born to her and her first husband Ivan. She loves classical music, tying quilts, and reading children's literature. After her husband's death, she taught elementary school in the Davis School District (Utah) for fifteen years to support her family. She later married El Dean Holliday, and they have served together in several Church callings and assignments, most recently as directors of Mormon Handcart Historic Sites in Wyoming.

Seek first the kingdom of God and all else shall be added unto you

WESTON GIBB HENRIE

I served in Denmark as a full-time missionary right after World War II. There were eight of us, and we were the first missionaries in that country after the war.

The Danes had suffered greatly. For example, their staple food was potatoes, and most people were not finding enough to feed their families. It was springtime, and they were still relying on last year's crop, which was dwindling fast.

A lady who was a member of the Church cooked for us. To our dismay, one morning she told us that she couldn't feed us anymore. She could not find enough potatoes to feed her own family plus our group of hungry missionaries. We had no idea how we were going to find enough food.

Then interesting things began to happen. While my companion and I were tracting the next day, I suddenly got a severe toothache. We needed to find a drugstore that carried what I needed for the pain.

After making inquiries, and after a pretty long walk, we found ourselves in an area we had never been in. We didn't find the drugstore, but I saw a train stopped on the railroad tracks nearby. A man was unloading a boxcar full of potatoes.

I said to my companion, "Let's see if that man would sell us some of those potatoes."

My companion replied, "Potatoes are rationed all over Denmark. He's not going to sell us any."

I felt it wouldn't hurt to at least ask. So we asked the man if he would sell us a hundred-pound sack of potatoes. The man hesitated at first but soon agreed. Then we asked if he would sell us another sack. The man looked at us strangely but agreed again. So we were able to buy two hundred pounds of potatoes.

We went back to show our treasure to the woman who had been cooking for us. Amidst the excitement, my toothache went away, though I had taken no medicine. It was my first and my last toothache. I have never had another toothache in my life.

Those sacks of potatoes fed the lady who had been cooking for us, her husband, and her two children, as well as keeping eight missionaries full until the new crop was harvested and the shortage was over.

Weston's career as a high school teacher influenced a generation of students who felt he gave them one of the most important educational experiences of their lives. His debate program was among the most successful in Utah. In addition to teaching, another of his great passions is horses. He served as president of the Cache Valley Quarter Horse Association and is well known for the show horses he has bred and trained. Now retired from teaching, he loves nothing more than to go out to the barn behind his home and spend precious time with his animal friends.

Pearl Harbor and the Price of Sugar

LAWRENCE CANTWELL

When Pearl Harbor was bombed, I was married and had two children. It was a Sunday morning, and I was at home. I worked at a grocery store, and the next day the phone rang constantly with people all asking the same question, "How much is sugar a pound?" And that's when the hoarding of goods began by those who could afford it. I knew this was going to happen. You see, I remembered World War I, and I was only six years old in 1917. I remember going through that war without any sugar on my mush. So all these phone calls didn't surprise me.

I think our government officials somehow knew in advance that the attack was coming because by the following Monday the ration books had already been printed and were ready to be given to the people of Cache Valley. All the other valleys were doing the same thing within a month's time.

Many of Lawrence's memories relate to food. No wonder. His father traveled a lot and his mother had poor health, so Lawrence pretty much raised himself. There was very little to eat around the house, so he rode his horse to the east bench of Cache Valley, near his hometown of Smithfield, and literally lived off what he found in the foothills. He ate "bushels" of sego lily bulbs, stinging nettle, wild raspberries, and strawberries. To avoid eating poisonous plants, Lawrence first offered a handful of an unknown plant to his horse. If the horse ate it, then Lawrence ate it. He says he never ate a leaf off a tree—they were always bitter to the taste.

Take your time to make important decisions

TED S. PERRY

I skipped a grade and graduated from high school at age seventeen. It seemed that everyone else was getting their draft notices to serve in World War II. I felt a great deal of peer pressure to join up. So, when my friends all marched down to the Navy office to enlist, I went with them. They said I needed my parents' signature, so we all went to Dad and Mother and explained the situation. My friends said they didn't want to leave me behind. So we presented the papers to be signed. My parents signed them. We were to report in thirty days, but as soon as I signed up that day at the Navy office, the man said, "Raise your right hand," and he gave me the oath right then and there. He said, "You're in the Navy now. We're leaving immediately for Ogden." From there we got on a train and left Utah, and I didn't get a chance to say good-bye to anybody.

I think I should have been a little more cautious. I was a priest at that time and hadn't yet been ordained an elder. As I went with the Navy and saw horrible things happen, I wondered if I had held the Melchizedek Priesthood, if things could have been a little bit better. I think if I had been more cautious and got things right with the Church first, I would have been happier.

Ted Perry is a retired lawyer and judge. He is a brother to Elder L. Tom Perry of the Quorum of the Twelve Apostles. He has served as a patriarch in Logan, Utah, for twenty-two years, a calling he loves. He says the oldest person to whom he has given a patriarchal blessing was ninety-seven years old.

The sweet scene of Daddy's return from the war

BETH FRANCIS TITENSOR

On December 7, 1941, I was nineteen years old and dating my future husband. It was a Sunday morning, and we were at a Church conference in Long Beach, California. A Brother Kirkham was conducting the meeting when someone came in and handed him a note. He stopped and said, "President Roosevelt has declared that we are in a state of war. All servicemen who are here are to report to their stations immediately." All these devoted sailors and soldiers in their uniforms stood up, went to the center aisle, and marched out.

Because of this event, we speeded up our marriage date. My husband was soon inducted into the Army. We were together just one year of the first four years of our marriage. During that time we became the parents of a little girl, Robin. During his absence I kept a picture of Dick in his uniform and told her that this was her daddy. So every time she saw a soldier she would say, "Oh, hi, Daddy!" When he did return home, a day early, she was asleep when he arrived, but when we walked down the hall past her bedroom, she woke up and sat up in bed. I said to her, "Robin, this is your daddy," and she said, "How do you do? I'm Robin Titensor."

Beth has served four missions for The Church of Jesus Christ of Latter-day Saints and hopes to go on a fifth. Each night before she goes to bed, she stands on her head for exercise, and every morning she does a shoulder stand. This is part of her yoga training, which she has used for many years. She also teaches a creative healing class every fall. Beth keeps active by canning fruit and jams in the summer, mows her own lawn, and reads two or three books at a time. Her future goals are to write her life history and her mother and father's love story. More immediately she plans to again climb her beloved Cove Mountain in northern Cache County, Utah.

Life is fragile—be grateful for it

BETTE SMITH KIRK

While my husband was in the U.S. Navy, we were stationed in Guam. One Saturday my husband and I had gone to the other side of the island with some of his friends. We found several underwater caves. We swam into the main cave for a picnic. I decided to stay there while my husband and our friends swam underwater through one passage cave to another cave. There seemed to be five caverns in all.

On the Monday morning after our visit, three Japanese soldiers surrendered to the authorities. They had been living in the same cave we had been in. Perhaps something in our conversations with each other, in that cave that day, communicated to them that the war was over. Possibly one or more of them knew English and could understand what we were saying. I was so grateful that they surrendered and that we were safe. It made me realize how fragile and special life on this earth really is.

Early in their marriage, Bette traveled all over the world with her husband, Kenneth Lloyd Kirk, because of his service in the Navy. They spent several years living in Guam and Germany. Later they moved to Smithfield, Utah, and lived there for more than thirty years. One nice thing about finally settling down and not traveling so much is that Bette can have a large photo gallery in her home where she proudly and lovingly displays the best photos she has of her family members. Bette has worked as a professional photographer for over thirty years.

My life was preserved for a purpose

NESTA PROVO

My first five years of life were war years—World War II. I remember hiding under the cupboard and under stairs and tables in the night when the bombs fell on London.

My first memories of Jesus were when I was three or four years old. We hid in the corners in the night while the bombs fell, with darkness everywhere. We kept the blackout curtains closed, and there was not a bit of light. The house was shaking and we were scared. I remember praying to Jesus and knowing that he would keep us alive. Our house was bombed many times with fire bombs but not so much with the explosives. The house caught on fire many times, but we were always kept safe during the war.

During those years of bombings and many other experiences, I always felt that I was meant to live and be preserved.

Nesta was born in Cardiff, Wales, and graduated from the University of Wales with a master's degree in linguistics. She was baptized a member of The Church of Jesus Christ of Latter-day Saints in the Mediterranean Sea in France by missionaries.

Losing a parent is very hard, but others looked out for us

CALVIN WATTS

Without question, the most difficult experience I had while growing up was when my mother died. I was in high school at that time. It was a very, very hard experience. My mother had received several priesthood blessings while she was battling cancer. The president of the temple came to our home and gave my mother a blessing to heal her. At that time in my life, I thought the blessing was supposed to *work*. It took me quite a while to understand why it didn't.

With my mother gone and my father working as a traveling salesman, I was pretty much on my own, although my younger sister Lucy was still at home. I had to learn to make a lot of big decisions by myself. I had to learn to cook, and I even learned to fry an egg. I signed my own report card at school and did lots of other things like that. Of course, the teachers could tell it was my handwriting, but they also knew my circumstances.

Looking back, I can see many times when the adults in the community showed me some extra patience and care. For example, several close friends and I liked to find a way to get into the old junior high school after the custodian had locked it up for the night. We loved finding a way in so we could play basketball. Sometimes we would jump in the swimming pool, but we didn't stay long because it was usually too cold. Sometimes I think we just wanted to be able to say we got in.

Years later, I saw the man who was the custodian of the old junior high school at the time I was a student. I told him, "Mr. Bench, you know there wasn't a time you locked up that school that we couldn't find a way to get in." Mr. Bench smiled and replied, "Did it ever occur to you that I might have purposely left you a way in?"

Calvin played basketball for Logan High School and very briefly at Utah State University. He was one of the youngest men to enlist in the U.S. Army Air Corps, at the age of eighteen. He was a pilot instructor and lieutenant in the United States Air Force at the age of nineteen, flying B-29 bombers in World War II. He married Ann Adams in 1944 at Davis-Montham Air Force Base in Tuscon, Arizona. They were sealed in the Logan Utah Temple in December 2002 after fifty-eight years of marriage. Calvin cofounded Cache Valley Builders Supply with his brothers Conley, Loy, and brother-in-law, Ace Raymond, in 1946. The business thrived for fifty-four years. Cal and Ann have three sons and two daughters. Cal has undergone two cardiac bypass surgeries, survived prostate cancer, and rebounded from a broken hip.

It's so hard to lose a parent, even if you are grown up

WILLIS "BILL" MCBRIDE

One spring day in 1968, I went to see how my father was doing. I stopped by his house in the morning, and he said he was going to burn some dry grass that day. I told him to wait and I would help him. I went back to his house later and could see that the whole lot had been burned. I called out to him but received no answer. I looked all through the house and found no one.

As I left the house, I could see something in the north part of the lot, up by the raspberry patch. I ran up there. It was Dad, lying on the ground. I remember saying, "Oh no! Dear God, no!" All his clothes were burned from him and his hair was burned off. I put my hand on his back. It was cold. I got in the car and went to tell my wife and daughter. I then called our family doctor. He said he would call the mortician. The mortician came but would not let us move Dad until the sheriff did an investigation. It had started to snow, and they did not get there until about 9 P.M. This really shook me up and tore me apart.

Dad was ninety-three and had lived a good and long life, but what a terrible way to go. Sometimes I wake up at night and picture him all burned like that. What a nightmare. He was a widower for eleven years and lived alone, taking care of himself and the home. He was very independent. He did not want to bother anyone. He always said things would turn out all right. That was one great lesson of faith we learned from him.

Bill had a fascination for local history. Having been born and raised in Hyrum, Utah, he read just about everything he could find on the history of that area. He started the Hyrum Museum, which was next door to his home. The museum had all kinds of historical artifacts, such as arrowheads, harnesses, musical instruments, and a variety of farm implements. Every Fourth of July, the McBride family would gather in Hyrum for the parade. Afterwards they would have a cookout in the McBrides' backyard, and then they would all walk next door and admire the museum, which would not exist without Willis "Bill" McBride.

Trials can bring us to a crisis of faith

JULIE RAPMUND JACOBS

While we were living in Indonesia, my husband, Rudolf Jacobs, an experienced pilot, was called into military action during World War II and was soon captured by the Japanese. I was pregnant with twins and had an infant son to care for. I struggled for the next three years to provide for my children. I sold knitting and other handiwork, trading everything I could to buy food. When Rudolf returned from a prisoner of war camp very sick and underweight, we decided to move to the Netherlands, where better medical help was available.

Six years later Rudolf was killed in a plane crash, and I was again left to provide for my family of four children ranging from ages five to fourteen. I worked teaching typing and shorthand. In 1960 I suffered another blow when my eldest son was killed in a car accident. Reeling under the loss, I experienced a crisis of faith. I couldn't understand why I had to go through this. I struggled to pray, but I found that I could not. Even though I had never attended a church, I had a strong belief in God. After a while I heard a voice that seemed to repeat, "Be still, God is love." I began to pray once more.

Not long afterward one of my sons was baptized into The Church of Jesus Christ of Latter-day Saints, followed by my sister and mother. But I was not yet convinced. The evening before my daughter was to be baptized, a missionary challenged me to pray in an effort to gain a testimony of the gospel. I did not promise the missionary anything, and when I said my prayers that night, I did not mention the Church. But in the middle of the night, I woke up with an urgent need to ask Father in Heaven if this was indeed the true Church where I could serve him.

Never had I prayed so sincerely or for so long. And never had I felt God's love and strength as I did on that night. When my prayer was over, I saw the sun shining through the curtains. As I gazed outside in the early morning hour, I felt a happiness and peace I had not known since before my son's death. I was baptized that day along with my daughter.

Julie was born in Semarang, Indonesia. Her father died when she was ten, and her Chinese mother, who had been disowned by her family for marrying a Dutchman, was unable to take care of her children. Julie lived with a foster family for several years until the family was reunited.

For twenty-one years Julie served in the Relief Society, including five years as Relief Society president of the Hague Netherlands Stake. Julie says, "Life isn't always easy, but our final reward will be that God will lovingly take us in his arms when we leave this world. I think about that, and it gives me the courage to accept the things that happen in my life."

I don't cry—I dance alone

SARAH "SADIE" BEEBE ELDER

When my husband was still alive, one day I was in the kitchen doing the dishes and the radio started playing a pretty song. My husband came in from the other room and grabbed me. We danced around the living room. Now that he is gone, when I hear a wonderful song on the radio, I don't cry—I dance alone, joyfully remembering him and the years we had together.

I feel that too many women carry guilt after their husbands die. I have some friends who say, "If only I had been nicer or told him I loved him more often." You can't change the past. The only things you can take with you are special moments and happy memories.

Looking on the bright side leaves no room for bitterness. All of us go through hard times. One friend who lost her husband told me, "There's no other woman who feels worse about losing her husband than I do. But I save my tears for my pillow." I try to make every day count joyfully. I overcome loneliness by being with a happy crowd. I don't have to rehash my husband's death. I accept life and live it.

Sadie Elder and her husband, known as Q, had six children—four girls and two boys. She was a Relief Society president for many years. Sadie said late in her life, "I know how I got into this life, but how do I get out of it?" Sadie Elder died at one hundred years of age.

Losing a spouse changes your whole life

RAMONA HINCKLEY SULLIVAN

You can't realize how much losing a spouse changes your life until it happens to you. You just have to have faith and make your own decisions. Someone has been making decisions with you all your married life. Now, you have to make decisions on money, where to go, where to live, what to do—alone. Everything about your whole life has changed. It will never be the same. You just get used to it. I don't think it gets any easier. But you do what you have to do.

Ramona's children and grandchildren adore her, referring to her as "a little woman full of love and energy." Every year as their children were growing up and later as marriages took place and grandchildren came along, Ramona and her husband, Patrick, faithfully gathered their posterity together and went on a summer vacation together. They bought a boat and often went to such places in the West as Lake Powell, Flaming Gorge, or Lake Tahoe. They also purchased a motor home, which made their family trips even more memorable. Certainly Patrick's death left a great void in their family circle.

On losing one's mate

VELOY BEYLE BUCKINGHAM

My husband and I almost made it to our fifty-first wedding anniversary. Now I have been a widow for thirteen years. To those who have lost their mates and are alone, I say, keep busy. Help other people. Keep your mind off yourself. And, most important, in managing your affairs, don't do anything in a hurry! Don't do anything for two years. Don't sell your house, don't move, or do anything big until you have time to really think about what you want to do.

Veloy met her future husband, Don, at the University of Idaho in Moscow, Idaho, where she was earning her teaching certificate. He had just finished a four-year stretch in the Navy after high school before going to the university. After dating during the summer of 1940, they were married in the Salt Lake Temple. They have two sons.

The right attitude will keep you young

ROSETTA THOMPSON WITTORF

My hair was fully gray by the time I turned forty. I always liked it and have never colored it. In those early days of being gray, I used to joke with my husband that someday someone would mistake me for his mother instead of his wife. We had laughed about it many times by the time it finally happened. I went into the optometrist's office in the medical building where my husband had his dental practice. The optometrist handed me my new glasses and said to me, "Oh, are you that nice Dr. Wittorf's mother—I mean, wife?" Realizing what he had said, he choked and blushed. Then he apologized. He looked at me with wonder when I burst out laughing. I told him he had made my day because my husband and I had been joking about this for a while! I told my husband, and we laughed and hugged. Now, I am ninety and love to tell everyone my age. I am proud of it, and I still think laughing keeps you young at heart.

Rosetta learned to play the piano as a child and was teaching other children by the time she was eleven years old. She and a childhood friend played duets on two pianos. She has played for Church meetings since her baptism forty-five years ago and has been the head organist at the Los Angeles California Temple since 1964. Even in her nineties, she organizes the schedule for all the organists for the Los Angeles California Temple.

Stay busy—both physically and mentally

CRAWFORD GATES

I heard a talk in church that when we receive the gift of the Holy Ghost, each of us receives other special gifts. At the age of eight it became apparent to me that music was my gift. I wrote my first piece when I was eight years old, not long after my baptism. I started the violin when I was nine and the viola when I was ten. Now I am in my eighties, and I have been writing music nearly every day since I was eight years old. That's a lot of sitting at the piano and a desk, composing and arranging.

The body needs exercise, so I have always taken a break from composition to make sure my body stays fit. I played tennis with my father when I was a teenager. I played tennis up to the age of eighty-four, with people who are twenty years younger than I was. Sometimes I beat them. I walk every morning and have gone swimming most of my life. And, to exercise my intellect, I read books and go to concerts and lectures. It is good to keep busy physically and mentally!

Composer, conductor, and educator, Crawford Gates is often referred to as the trailblazer for today's Mormon media composers. He started early, offering his talent and service to his local home ward where, at the age of ten, Crawford started serving as the ward Primary accompanist. For the next seventy-plus years, Crawford's name became something of a legend in Utah. He became a mentor to a group of LDS composers and performers seeking to contribute original music to LDS popular and classical music.

No fear of the future

CLARK L. PUFFER

I have been a teacher and school administrator most of my life. I'm not afraid of dying. At different times in my life, I was probably afraid of dying, but not now. Dying is just another new assignment. I'm not ready for that new assignment, but if that divine person who writes up the curriculum gives me that new assignment, then that's OK.

Although retired, Clark is still helping others in education. He is an advisor at Utah State University for interns who are working on their master's degree in education or on their administration certificate. The greatest thing about retirement, according to Clark, is doing what he wants to do, such as traveling. "I'm interested in the world. I believe I have been to almost all the continents in the world." And yet, he feels it's just as much fun to take his wife to the movies.

Children and dogs are great judges of character

ANN ENGLAND BARKER

I'm proud of my wrinkles and gray hair. I've earned every one of them. Which way do the lines in your face turn, up or down? When you are old, your face shows who you really are.

Do children and dogs like you? If so, it's a compliment. They are great judges of character.

Overcome your weaknesses and faults while you're young, because if you don't, they may be all that's left as you grow old.

Ann Barker's dreams have been fulfilled, all of them, she says, but usually too late or when they don't matter anymore. She has traveled, received a college education after forty, and has a lovely home that is a reflection of her personality.

Keep moving!

THORA HALES MECHAM

I was born the same year the *Titanic* sank! Although my eyesight is poor, I listen to a wide range of books on tape, especially the scriptures. And I don't take any medication or pills. I know a lot of people who have a whole handful of pills they have to take, but I don't. And most important, I keep moving! I can walk around this assisted living building faster than any resident here, with the exception of a sixty-five-year-old man that just moved in. He beats me by just a little.

Thora's morning always begins with personal prayer. She says, "I do as Brigham Young said to do. I don't take any food into my mouth until I pray." Then, when she's not busy clocking the speed of her morning walk around the retirement center, Thora loves to visit with others and remembers fondly the forty years she taught school.

Turn everything over to the Lord

JOAN GROESBECK

I lived my younger years liking myself for what I accomplished. I was a great student with a thirst for knowledge. I was a hard-working teacher. I was a Relief Society president and the bishop's wife. I was an involved mother, raising my sons, who all have doctorate degrees. I am proud of all of these things.

But, in my older years, I have learned to value myself as a daughter of God. I can no longer accomplish all of the things I used to. The most perfect day in my life was the day I became a mother. A perfect day now would be a day when I am not in pain.

I have finally allowed myself to recognize that I am learning a new lesson in life, which is, that it is OK to let others help me as I have helped those before me. I know my Heavenly Father loves me even when I stop to take a nap or accept service. I would hope others could learn the lesson of giving up control and turning everything over to the Lord more easily than I have.

Joan graduated from Brigham Young University and taught English at East High School in Salt Lake City. She has lived in Pasadena, California, for thirty years. She has sixteen grandchildren and one great-grandchild.

I still feel the need to apologize

MELBA SIMMONS JOHNSON

Although I look back on my life with gratitude and satisfaction, I also have some regrets, one in particular. I remember when I was in school, I was asked to write an essay about my family. In it I said my mother was not a good cook. When she read it, I saw the hurt in her eyes. I regretted it immediately and still see the look on her face to this day. Now I cook just like she did. Someday, I will apologize to her when I get to the other side.

Melba was born and raised in Oklahoma. The author of two books, As I Remember *and* This and That, *she has also published articles in numerous magazines, including* Reminisce. *She continues a long-standing family tradition of cooking a nice Sunday dinner for her children and grandchildren. Melba was once asked what day in her life was the most wonderful day she has had so far. She answered with no hesitation, "The day our twins were born!"*

We do the best we can

MARIE ARRINGTON DAVIDSON

When you get to be my age, which is eighty-eight, you look back and see that life brings both highs and lows to everyone. Do I have any regrets when I look back on my life? Well, I suppose I can see times I could have behaved differently or chosen a different path to follow. But I also know I've done the best that I knew how with the knowledge that I had at the time, and it does me absolutely no good to regret anything.

At the same time, I see days where I've had experiences that were absolutely wonderful—perfect days that I would love to live over again if given the chance. Some of those precious times include days when I have attended the temple and watched my own family members be baptized for our relatives who did not have the opportunity to hear the gospel while they were here on the earth. I love being surrounded by family members, and to be able to do that work in one of the Lord's temples is as good as it gets.

Marie grew up near Twin Falls, Idaho, and has spent much of her life researching the names of her ancestors. For her it is much more than a hobby; it is a passion that never lets up. Almost from scratch she has constructed her family tree, using skills that qualify her as a registered professional genealogist. She has done considerable work for others who have hired her to solve particularly difficult research problems. Her beloved husband, Bud, shares her interest, and together they have brought the blessings of the temple to thousands of souls who have awaited the ordinances of the gospel.

I SHOULD HAVE BEEN MORE GENTLE

D. PETER LASSIG, SR.

One of my regrets is that there have been times in my life when I could have been more gentle with people and even with animals.

For example, there was a worker in the LDS Church purchasing department where I worked. I felt that she was too slow in obtaining something we needed. I was frustrated and told her boss. When I saw her again, she looked at me with such a hurt feeling.

I felt as bad about that as I did about killing a rabbit years ago. I was on a hunting trip with my brother when I killed the rabbit. It cried like a baby before it died. That hurt me so badly that I decided I would never shoot another living thing again.

In both instances I should have been gentler. The truth is that all living things are created by God. We are here on this beautiful earth to learn how to be more like our Father in Heaven. I should have been more like him, being more gentle with co-workers, with the rabbit, and indeed with all living things.

Peter says, "On marriage, I'd give the same advice that Spencer Tracy gave Katharine Hepburn: 'Know your lines, and don't bump into the furniture.' The second piece of advice is to do well in English. If you can't communicate, the dream you dream will be yours alone to enjoy. In finding a spouse, you better be good. Sometimes it happens suddenly, intensely, and unexpectedly. I told a young man who was struggling with his first year of marriage, 'You need to look at your wife and consider what she says to you as if it were instructions straight from the throne of God. If you will do exactly as she asks, never going halfway but always 100 percent of the way, you will be successful in your marriage.'"

Don't wait too long to ask about your ancestry

RICHARD CUDDY HOWE

One of my greatest regrets is that I didn't take the opportunity to talk more to my parents about their parents and other family members who are now long gone. I have so many questions now, if only I had even a few minutes with some of them! This is a common thing with young people. They're more interested in today than yesterday. I guess I always felt that there was plenty of time later to talk about their earlier lives. When I grew up, however, I became much more interested in family history and those kinds of things almost overnight. But it was too late. That is one of my biggest regrets.

Richard may feel that he didn't take the time to ask about his family history, but he has given a lifetime of public service that would, in fact, place his own name in the Utah history books. In addition to a successful law practice in Salt Lake County, he served in the Utah House of Representatives, where he became Speaker of the House, and then six years in the Utah Senate. In 1980 he was appointed a justice of the Utah Supreme Court; he later was appointed chief justice. He is the only person in Utah history to serve as a member of the State House of Representatives, the State Senate, and the State Supreme Court.

Don't wait to express love

MARILYN EAMES BAKER

Of course I have regrets. I regret not acting on certain feelings I had that I should call someone in need. I also remember wishing I had gotten more information from my grandfather and gotten closer when visiting with him or when visiting with my father, who eventually died of cancer. My father was expressing his concerns to me, and I said, "You're going to be all right," and I let it go at that. But I really didn't express my feelings for him at that time. Above all, don't wait to express love.

One of Marilyn's lifelong dreams that she was never able to fulfill was to receive her nursing degree. She was a young mother of two and a nurse's aide. It was all she could do then to keep up with the other demands upon her time. Today, she loves to read, especially Church books, and when David, her husband, leaves the house, she turns on the television or radio. "I like friendly noise while I'm working. I don't like a quiet house."

What do you do when you think no one is watching?

J. L. JAUSSI

After high school I stayed out of school for one year and worked at the Budge Ranch to get enough money to go to college. It was during this winter that I had my first real trip away from home.

At the age of seventeen, I was sent to California to deliver a load of cattle from the ranch. There were some highly respected church men from the valley who also had cattle on the same train. We rode together in the caboose for three days. In California they offered me coffee and took me to a burlesque show. I knew it was wrong, but I didn't know how to handle it. It was quite an eye-opener to me to see what men will do when they think no one is watching. And I learned I have to be responsible for my actions.

J. L. remembers another unfortunate circumstance that took place in his fourth-grade class. The students were having a class party. "Some of the elite of the class, as they thought of themselves, chased me from the party. I will never forget the long walk home for me, all alone, without a friend in the world. The sad part was that the teacher was right beside me in the gymnasium. He heard and knew all that was going on and seemed to concur with it." Since that time J. L. has spent twenty-three years as a teacher, being very careful that if he could help it, no one in his school was ever treated that way or had those feelings.

Hold your tongue—you won't be sorry

COLLEEN HINCKLEY MAXWELL

I've never held my tongue and been sorry. There have indeed been a few times I've said something I've later been sorry for. It's so much easier to not say anything and not be sorry than to say something and have to agonize over it.

Colleen Hinckley was born and reared in Salt Lake City. She graduated from the University of Utah in homemaking education. After teaching at a school in Arizona, she married Neal A. Maxwell, who later became a member of the Quorum of the Twelve Apostles. Her husband described her as a "kind of Gibraltar—someone who can be tough and strong in the storms of life." She continues to provide quiet, thoughtful service to her extended family and her neighbors.

Stay out of debt and be prepared

NORA COOK DUNCAN

The Great Depression of 1929 hit my family in the fall about the time school was to start. On a Saturday morning my sisters Florence and Ethel and Father and I went into Ogden to shop. I bought a new hat to wear to teachers' institute and a Bamberger train ticket book so I could ride to school. I also cashed a check so I could pay for my board and have about twenty dollars on hand. Florence, who was working for the Del Monte factory peeling tomatoes, also cashed her check.

While we were shoppin,g Father went into the Ogden State Bank to deposit the check he had received from the sale of his wheat harvest the fall before. He always kept the wheat harvested one year until after the next year's harvest was finished. I think the check must have been well over five hundred dollars. While he waited for us, he visited with his friend who was president of the bank. This man assured my father that the bank was in no danger of closing. Two days later, after he had deposited his annual income on the assurance of his friend, the bank closed.

The following Monday we received word that the bank had closed its doors. In my memory I see father sitting in a chair, his head in his hands, with tears in his eyes. All of his hard-earned money had been in that bank. He sat there for a long time and then lifted his head and said, "We will get along. Thank the Lord we don't owe anyone a penny."

Indeed we did get along, because we had plenty of home-grown canned food to eat. We had an orchard and a garden; we dried our fruit and bottled our beans, peas, and corn. We raised our own meat and had our wheat ground into flour. We baked all our bread and churned our own butter. We made pickles, chili sauce, jams, and jellies. When we needed sugar, salt, etc., we bought them at Mr. Casper's little horse-drawn store on wheels that came from Ogden once a week. Mother traded her homemade butter and eggs for other things she needed.

After the Depression, the bank settled its claims, and we received only fifty cents for every dollar we had in the bank. We learned great lessons from that experience.

Bright-eyed and inquisitive, Nora was ever a student and a teacher. She loved to study the gospel, nature, new places and cultures, history, literature, and poetry. She taught in elementary school for nine years and in Church auxiliaries for fifty-four. She was a talented homemaker and gardener. Delicate violets, beautiful roses, delicious peaches, and friends and family thrived under her watchful and tender care. When she died at age ninety-eight, friends came from all over the United States and Canada to pay their respects to this wonderful woman. Many were former missionaries who had served in South Africa with Nora and her husband, Leroy, who was mission president.

After a big disagreement, repent and go find your mate

J. L. JAUSSI

We lived in Oceanside, California. I was a lieutenant in the military at the time. My wife and I had an argument there. It was quite a fight. There was a lot of tension back and forth. I don't remember most of what I said to her, but I finally told her, "I'm getting out of here." I went down to the beach and pondered my actions. I thought, What's the matter with you, you dumbbell? So, I headed back, and as I looked up the path, I saw her coming my way. It was wonderful that each of us was coming to find the other. That was the end of it. No more fighting.

J. L. and Marilyn Jaussi have celebrated sixty-five years together as husband and wife. J. L. looks back on the years gone by and says, "Our lives together have been exceptional." They have five children, twenty-five grandchildren, and fifty-four great-grandchildren. Between his time in the military and his work later as district coordinator of seminaries for The Church of Jesus Christ of Latter-day Saints, they have traveled the world. J. L. started the first seminary and institute programs in Australia as well as in the midwestern United States.

Eat wisely and relax!

LAWRENCE CANTWELL

I think my age, ninety-six, comes from my Irish genes. And I also think foods you eat stay with you for a long time. I believe the foods I ate as a youth are still with me, even the wild things I ate in the mountains. I've never tasted chicken or poultry. I eat hardly any meat. I don't like seeing loads of cattle being killed for man to consume.

As far as keeping my mind alert, I believe sometimes you need to turn yourself loose and go roam, and sometimes that means getting away from people. Go to the mountains. Be alone once in a while. Ponder. Stress today is killing people.

Lawrence always wanted to climb Mt. Everest. Instead, he climbed to within one thousand feet of the top of the Grand Tetons. In fact, he did it twice, once at eighty-seven and again at eighty-nine. The high altitude affected him adversely; otherwise, he would have made it to the top. He had had a desire to be a brain surgeon, which would have taken him to Vienna, Austria, for his studies, but a man named Adolph Hitler put an end to that.

A husband's promise comes true

WILLIAM AND CLARA DANIELS

AS TOLD BY NORA COOK DUNCAN

My husband was called to preside over a mission in South Africa in 1952. In 1954 our mission was visited by President David O. McKay, the first Church president or general authority to visit there. One evening he spoke in Cape Town, and Elder Barry Mayo, my husband's counselor in the mission presidency, took Sister Clara Daniels and her daughter, Sister Alice Okkers, to church to hear him. After that very spiritual meeting, President McKay went into the cultural hall to greet everyone. When he shook hands with Sister Daniels, he said, "God bless you."

When we went to find the two sisters to take them home, Sister Daniels was sitting on a bench in the chapel, weeping. Someone said, "Sister Daniels, why are you crying? This is a happy time."

She said, "I never thought I'd live to see the day when a prophet of the Lord would shake this old black hand of mine. Think of it! The prophet shook this old black hand of mine!"

Sister Daniels then shared a sacred story about her husband:

In the early 1900s, William Daniels, a well-educated black man, was taught the gospel in Cape Town, South Africa. He knew the Church was true, but before he would join, he traveled to Salt Lake City to meet with President Joseph F. Smith to discuss why the blacks couldn't hold the priesthood at that time. Brother Daniels was satisfied with what he learned and was baptized on May 30, 1915, in

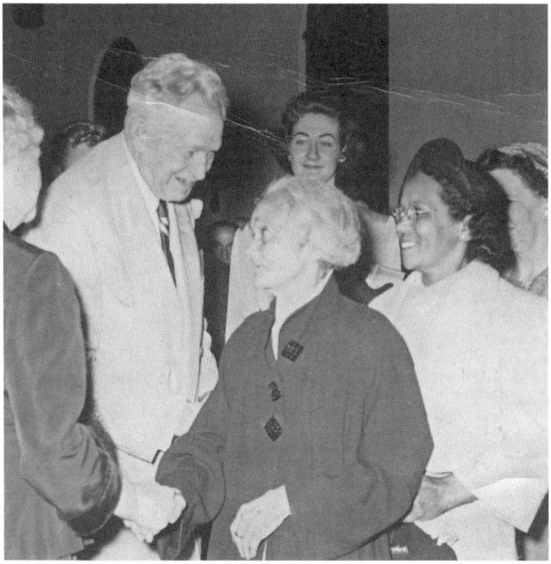

Utah. He returned to Cape Town, and his wife and all their children were baptized

Then Sister Daniels told us that before her husband died, he told her to stay close to the Church. He said that if she remained faithful, the day would come when she would be blessed to see the prophet of the Lord. She said she wondered at the time how a poor old black lady would be able to get the money to travel to Salt Lake City so she could see the prophet. She wondered how that promise could ever come true. But now she had seen the prophet. President McKay had come to Cape Town, and he had shaken her hand. Her tears were tears of joy. Her husband's promise had been fulfilled.

After Nora and her husband, Leroy, returned home to Utah from their missionary service in South Africa, they remained in touch with many of the missionaries who had served with them. Every year the Duncans hosted a mission reunion at their home in Centerville, Utah, which was attended by seventy-five to one hundred missionaries and their spouses. When Nora passed away at age ninety-eight, friends came from all over the United States and Canada to attend her funeral and pay tribute to this remarkable woman.

Testimony of the Book of Mormon

Beth Francis Titensor

We lived up in Ogden Canyon for a summer while my husband, Dick, worked for the Bureau of Reclamation. We lived in a little trailer. While I was there I started to read the Book of Mormon. As I read on, these men and women of the Book of Mormon just came alive to me. I felt like I really knew them! And I knew the Book of Mormon was true before I got to the very end.

This testimony was confirmed and strengthened by a powerful spiritual experience that followed. It was a bright moonlit night, and there was a trail that went to a big rock which overlooked the canyon. I hiked up there in the moonlight and sat on the rock. I poured out my heart to the Lord. I thanked him for the Book of Mormon and thanked him for Lehi and Nephi and all the wonderful people from that time. As I was praying, with tears of gratitude, it was as if my whole being was filled with light. There was no darkness in me at all, and the Holy Ghost bore witness to me that it was true. I knew that God knew that I knew, and that's where I really gained my testimony.

Since her husband's death in 1986, Beth has served four missions for The Church of Jesus Christ of Latter-day Saints: a proselyting mission in Tampa, Florida; a temple mission in Atlanta, Georgia; a Deseret Industries mission in Preston, Idaho; and most recently, a temple mission to Ecuador. Beth has been a vegetarian for more than thirty years. She also practices yoga, which she feels has kept her remarkably physically fit and spiritually alert. "A perfect day" for this mother of seven would be to get up early and hike up to her "sacred grove near Cove, Utah, and have a talk with the Lord." She then would return home to fix breakfast for her family and spend the rest of the day working in the soil in her yard.

Ask the Lord if it is true

TED S. PERRY

I got the measles when I was in the third grade. With the red measles, you're not supposed to read. My mother put me up in the bedroom and darkened the room. She said, "Now you can't read. You've just got to lie here until you get over the measles."

After she closed the door, I started rummaging around the room. My brother, who is Elder L. Tom Perry of the Quorum of the Twelve Apostles, has always been very religious, and he kept a Book of Mormon under the mattress of the bed we both slept in. My mother didn't know the book was there. I read the Book of Mormon all the way through. I came to the last part where it said you can test this book and ask the Lord if it is true or not. So I knelt down and asked the Lord. The confirmation came, and I've never doubted it since. I was eight years old and had just been baptized.

Ted served a full-time mission for The Church of Jesus Christ of Latter-day Saints in the East Central States Mission. He successfully practiced law for thirty-six years and was a municipal court judge for eleven years. Ted has served as a patriarch in Logan, Utah, for twenty-two years, a calling he loves.

Living, beautiful flowers testify of the Resurrection

PEGGY CHRISTENSEN BREWER HOLLIDAY

My husband Ivan loved flowers. Though frugal with his money, flowers were the one thing he could not resist splurging on a little. In 1983, after many crippling years of arthritis, he contracted leukemia, triggered by the potent drugs required to ease pain in his body. That fall before his death he secretly bought more than two hundred flower bulbs, mostly tulips. He planted these all along the side and front of the house. The winter was especially cold that year, but it wasn't just the weather that was cold, as his chair at the dinner table was left vacant a few days after Christmas.

In January Ivan was in and out of consciousness in his University of Utah Hospital bed. He knew he wouldn't be coming home again. Shortly before his death he confessed to me his somewhat frivolous flower purchase of the previous fall. Then he continued with these words, "If those small bulbs can lie all winter long in the frozen earth and then in the spring somehow find the strength and courage to rise up out of that hard ground and blossom, I too can rise again. And this coming spring, when your garden is full of flowers, think of me and know that we will be together again."

Ivan died the last day of January. In the spring the expected flowers filled the beds. It is not just sentiment that caused me to say that the flowers were more beautiful that year than they ever were before. Tulips bloomed in brilliant colors, and each flower was a celebration of life and renewal. They reminded our family that our heartbreaking loss would not be forever. My husband will one day be with us again.

Peggy's first husband, Ivan Brewer, died January 31, 1984. Together they had five children. After her husband's death, she taught elementary school in the Davis School District (Utah) to support her family. She later married El Dean Holliday, father of two, whose wife had died. Together they have sixteen grandsons and one granddaughter. They served an eighteen-month mission to Athens, Greece, and later served in the Logan Utah Temple for three years, El Dean as a member of the temple presidency and Peggy as assistant to the matron. They also spent two years as directors of Mormon Handcart Historic Sites in Wyoming. Peggy loves classical music, tying quilts, and reading children's literature.

Find answers in the scriptures

THORA HALES MECHAM

Man cannot be saved in ignorance. I have always had an inquiring mind. If I had a question, I would always go and find the scriptures and study them. I read the Book of Mormon when I was sixteen years old. It didn't hit me all at once, but my testimony gradually grew from then on. I've never doubted that the Church was true, not for one minute. When you have the kind of father and mother I had, you trust, learn from them, and believe. Once, during a testimony meeting, my mother stood and spoke in tongues, after which another woman stood and interpreted and then testified that the things that my mother said were true.

Thora Mecham's typical day starts with getting up and saying her prayers. She said, "I do like Brigham Young said. I don't take any food in my mouth until I pray." Because of her poor eyesight, Thora listens to tapes of the Book of Mormon, Ensign, *Church books,* Reader's Digest, *and even magazines on tapes—without the advertisements, which is fine with her. She is interested in public affairs. She believes that everyone should be actively engaged in the welfare of their communities. Years ago she met Ronald Reagan while attending the State Republican Convention in Salt Lake City. She proclaims, "I'm a Republican and proud of it!"*

My most perfect day

MELLA PETERSON WILKINSON

My most perfect day is every day I wake up! When I wake up, my habit is to look up at the ceiling and say, "Yippee!"

My niece and nephew stayed with me one time. When they heard me, they said, somewhat surprised, "Why do you do that, Aunt Mella?"

And I said, "Because I am grateful for this day. I'm grateful for this life." Even now I still wake up and say, "Yippee."

My son is gradually getting used to it now, but the first few times he heard me, he'd say, "What are you doing in there?"

"Well," I told him, "this is the way I wake up every morning. I feel so grateful that even before I say my prayers or get out of bed, I yell, "Yippee."

Mella was married to James Clynn Wilkinson for forty-two years before he passed away in 1975. They moved to Portland, Oregon, shortly their first child was born. People of all ages love to be around Mella because of her positive attitude and enthusiasm for life. As she walks into any social setting, people surround her to give her a hug and visit a while. Although she is in constant pain on account of her back, she always has a smile to share, and she shows genuine concern for other people.

Contributors